Start Programming with PHP

An Introduction to PHP and MySQL

Table of Contents

Changes to Server2Go for MySQL
PHP .INI File Configuration
Apache Configuration
IIS Configuration
List of Built-in Functions
List of Escape sequences

Projects

Register Your Copy
If you email me your comments on the book or just say, "Hey, I bought your book.", as I develop material I will forward it to you. Lesson Plans, Projects, additional chapters, quiz questions, videos, are all in the various stages of development. Help me keep your book current and useful in the classroom. I promise I will not sell or give your email address or distribute it, or sell it. It will only be used for me to contact you about new material. My email address is: jkelley742@gmail.com My web site is: http://www.gurus4pcs.com

INTRODUCTION

For years, I have been teaching a course that introduces PHP programming. I decided to put my notes on paper in a form that would serve as a text for the lessons of the course, in the order and the way I teach.

I have had success with my approach and I hope all who use this in their classes or for their own self study, find it worthwhile.

As a user and proponent of Open Source Software, this book was written in its entirety using OpenOffice.org. I used Writer to convert it to a PDF for distribution.

FOR THE INSTRUCTOR:

One of the most frustrating parts of teaching computer related subjects is the books. There are many good books on many subjects. However, I find that for some courses I don't need 24 chapters on a topic that force my instruction into that chapter pattern or sequence. Often I would like a few chapters or even sections from a book, arranged in my sequence, and supplemented by my notes to create a lesson or part of a course.

PHP textbooks available are many and varied, for the most part quite good. But, I just needed a few basic lessons to allow me to introduce Computer Studies majors to the basic concepts of PHP programming. Also, I am fighting the tendency to teach the way I learned, with long laborious lectures on theory. I find that today's student suffers from what I call "The Sesame Street Syndrome". That is learning in 5 to 10 minute segments in an entertaining way. So, now we must adjust to the new paradigm of teaching and learning. I began this work in an attempt to match this learning pattern. Small segments of lessons with lots of hands on activities.

FOR THE STUDENT:

I teach at a small community college that has kept tuition low. We serve a rural community and most of our students, as in other community colleges are on some type of financial aid. One day in the bookstore I totaled up the cost of two books for a course I was teaching and found that the books cost more than the tuition. No wonder I had students that shared a book or worse yet, did not purchase the book. Those books were not that good that they were worth more than thirteen weeks of instruction. Yes, they had a test bank (often with mistakes), they had the usual tiresome PowerPoint slides (often with mistakes), an instructor manual that, somehow, never fit the way I teach the course and some data files that went with the lab exercises (most I never used). All packed in the book and a CD.

SUPPLEMENTS:

It is my intention to supplement this book with a web page. This way I can provide updates to the material on a moments notice. We are teaching in a field where change is good, frequent and where printed copy does not stand the test of time. Test banks while nice, often leave the instructor explaining why a question was wrong. Sometimes I have found that I agree with the student and have no rationale as to why the test bank had a different answer. So, don't expect big fancy test banks. Perhaps some questions that I use in my classes but in a format the instructor can modify to their own satisfaction. Programming Exercises as I come up with new

4

material would be included in a supplemental web page. Once again, use what you like or make your own. PowerPoint slides, why? Students usually sleep through them and then want to print them out. If you really need them, make your own as you prepare your lesson. Better yet, use CamStudio or Jing (for free) to create a short lesson. Use YouTube and make a movie and post it to make a point.

SUMMARY

I am a computer programmer who turned teacher. I see a need in my own classroom for a text with lots of examples that take a student through creating PHP programs, step by step. Hands on is the way to learn programming and this text is designed to facilitate the students hands on experience. This text gives the theory in text for reference or reading, then examples written to lead a student through practicing the theory with step by step examples. So, here is my attempt to teach PHP Programming, Step-by-Step.

Start Programming with PHP

An Introduction to PHP and MySQL

LESSON 1: Getting Started

Lesson 1.1 – PHP Environment Setup

Before we begin practicing our PHP exercises, it is necessary to install some software on our computer.

- A Web Server – PHP will work with all Web Server software. The most common web servers are Microsoft's IIS and Apache. We will concentrate on using Apache Web Server as it can be obtained for free from apache.org. It is also part of all of the packages discussed in the remainder of this lesson.
- PHP - The PHP parser must be installed. It is part of all packages discussed in the remainder of this lesson but may also be installed independently by obtaining it for free from php.com.
- A Database - Again, PHP works with most database software. In our lessons we will address only the MySQL database. It is part of all of the packages discussed in the remainder of this lesson and again, it is Free.

While all three components can be downloaded for free, separately, and installed, I highly recommend that you use one of the **LAMP** packages available. These packages include a complete testing environment, that can be installed easily, without major configuration issues. These packages are available for Windows, Linux and Mac operating systems.

The acronym **LAMP** stands for the combination of **L**inux, **A**pache, **M**ySQL and **P**HP. This combination makes up a complete development package for PHP and MySQL. The Apache, MySQL and PHP packages are standard for all operating systems. These packages run on one or more of the standard operating systems, Windows, Mac and Linux. Study each of the available packages and find the best one for your operating system and environment.

Another alternative is to obtain web hosting service that supports PHP and MySQL and use the host server to do your development and testing. While this can be done, it is not recommended as it will be difficult for the beginning PHP programmer to debug programs.

Four different packages will be reviewed in this lesson. Each of these packages have been used by the author and they will work. WampServer is most useful for a Windows installation on a laptop or desktop that will be the only workstation used for the development of PHP programs. Server2Go can be installed on your flash drive and excellent for those who will be working on several different computers. XAMPP works well on Windows, Linux and Mac. It works the same on each device and if you are not a Windows user, an excellent choice. Lastly, WOS is another version for your flash drive. Not as robust as Server2Go but certainly an alternative.

Yes, there are some others but they have not been included as they have not been tested by the author. They will probably work with all examples as Apache, PHP and MySQL are all well tested cross platform programs.

Lesson 1.2 - Install and Use WAMPSERVER

Wampserver is designed to be installed and run on the Windows Operating System. First, it is necessary to obtain a current copy of the WampServer software and install it on your computer. Download the software from http://www.wampserver.com. Double click on the downloaded file and just follow the instructions. Everything is automatic. The WampServer package is delivered with the latest releases of Apache, MySQL and PHP.

The functions of Wampserver are easy to use so it should not be necessary to explain them in detail.

Left click on the Wampserver icon to:
- manage your Apache and MySQL services
- switch online/offline (give access to everyone or only localhost)
- install and switch Apache, MySQL and PHP releases
- manage servers settings
- access logs
- access settings files
- create alias

Right click on the Wampserver icon to:
- change WampServer's menu language
- access a help page

Once the install is complete, you are ready to use PHP.

Figure 1.2.1

Click on the wampserver icon, select localhost and you should see the following page in the browser you selected during the install.

Figure 1.2.2

Wampserver is available from http://www.wampserver.com/en/

Lesson 1.3 – Install and Use server2go

A web server that runs out of the box. No installation required. Run it off your hard drive, run it off your memory stick, CD-RW, SD card or external hard drive. Configuration of Apache, PHP or MySQL not required.

Main Features
- FREE
- Run from HD, CD, SD, USB
- Full featured web server
- Includes many PHP extensions
- Supports MySQL databases
- Supports SQLite databases
- Supports PHP and Perl
- Runs on Windows 98 and above

Installation
- Download File
- Unzip
- Place all PHP scripts, HTML pages, images in the htdocs directory.
- MySQL databases are placed in the dbdir directory.

Now, you are ready to use Server2Go. In the extracted server2go directory, there is a server2go application file. Double click on this file and you should see the following page displayed in your default browser. This page is found in the htdocs directory and is named index.php DO NOT DESTROY THIS FILE!

Figure 1.3.1

The links on the left side of this page gives you access to:
- SAMPLES
  - PHP Information
  - GD-Lib Test
  - SQLite Test
  - MySQL Test
- TOOLS
  - phpMyAdmin
- License
  - License
  - Make a Donation
- Links
  - Forum
  - Wiki

I recommend that you rename this file from index.php to oldindex.php. This preserves the file and allows me to use the index.php or index.html names in development. When Server2Go starts you will get an the directory of the htdocs file displayed. When you want to run the main screen just select oldindex.php and double-click. As you see there are numerous folders shown in the Figure 1.3.2 below.

Figure 1.3.2

To shutdown, close the browser. You will get a pop up message "closing server".

Server2go is available from http://www.server2go-web.de

Lesson 1.4 – Install and Use XAMPP

An easy to install Apache distribution containing PHP, Perl, MySQL, PHPMyAdmin. Just download, extract and install. XAMPP is available for Windows, Linux Mac OS X, and Solaris. Best of all, it's FREE!

The Windows version comes in two flavors. A distribution that requires installation, and one that you just unzip and run. The latter can be run from a USB drive, SD card or external drive.

XAMPP Lite requires 17MB for the self-extracting zip file and 118 MB for the extracted files. The Lite package contains Apache, PHP, MySQL, phpMyAdmin, Openssi and SQLite. This is sufficient for the purposes of this tutorial.

The XAMPP version also contains FileZilla FTP server, PEAR, ADOdb, Mercury Mail Transport System, Webalizer, Zend Optimizer, XAMPP control panel and XAMPP security. If you are running this from one computer, this is the optimal environment for development and management of more sophisticated development.

To install XAMPP Lite go to the apachefriends website, find the Windows version of the self extracting file and download it. Run and extract the contents to the root directory of your hard drive, flash drive, etc..

Test your installation by navigating to the **xampplite** directory in the root of the installation drive. Start the Apache Server by running the **apache_start.bat** file. Then we can test the server by typing: http://localhost/ into the address bar of your favorite browser.

10

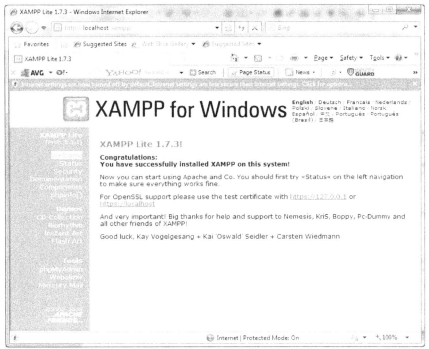

Figure 1.4.1

To stop all Apache processes you run the **apache_stop.bat** file in the **xampplite** directory.

XAMPP is available from http://www.apachefriends.org

There is also a version oc XAMPP that will run on PortableApps. This is a runtime environment for a USB, cloud or any removable device. It allows for the installation of numerous programs, some in a limited size or function that will go with you as your portable office.

PortableApps in available from http://www.portableapps.com

Lesson 1.5 – Install and Use WOS

Webserver On a Stick (WOS) is an Apache server based on PHP and MySQL. It is portable on a USB stick, external drive or SD card. It should be installed and run from the root directory of the drive on which it was installed. Simply download, unzip and run.

Figure 1.5.1

The following screen should show on start:

Figure 1.5.2

The WOS screen should look like this:

Figure 1.5.3

If you get the message "old.dir not writeable" it can be fixed by:
> open old.dir in a text editor
> copy the contents to another file
> delete the old file
> save the new file as old.dir

WOS is availble from http://wos-portable.en.softonic.com.

Lesson 1.6 – Summary

With all these choices and I'm sure there are more out there, what should you install? I prefer to have one that runs off my USB memory stick. I can take it between all of the machines that I work on and do my development and testing. If you are working on projects in many different places on different machines it is probably the best choice to use Server2Go, XAMPP or WOS. I have used all three and all work. Which is better? I'll leave that up to you. If you are serious about development you will try them all before making up your mind. I have my favorites.

All of the examples in this book were done and tested using Server2Go.

In Review:

1.   The product that runs on Windows, Linux and Mac is:
    a.   Wampserver
    b.   Server2Go
    c.   XAMPP
    d.   WOS
2.   The acronym LAMP stands for:
    a.   Linux And MySQL PHP
    b.   Live Apache MySQL PHP
    c.   Linux Archive MySQL Perl
    d.   Linux, Apache, MySQL, PHP
3.   The most used Web Server that runs on multiple platforms:
    a.   Apache
    b.   IIS
    c.   Linux
    d.   Tuxedo

An Introduction to PHP and MySQL

LESSON 2: Basics of PHP

Lesson 2.1 - PHP Syntax

The first thing to note about PHP is that it is not generally case sensitive. Most programmers stick to lowercase for programming.   Since PHP is used to generate HTML and HTML tags should always be written in lowercase, let's stick with lowercase for most of our code and only use uppercase for emphasis.

A PHP script or program is generally in one of three forms:

```
<?php    --php code--   ?>
<?        --php code--   ?>
<script language="php">  --php code--   </script>
```

All three will work for your programs. This book will use the first form for all examples. It seems to be the most common form used.

A semicolon (;) is the statement terminator. A semicolon must appear at the end of each statement in the program.

The echo() function is one of the most commonly used PHP statement. It is used to display the argument inside the parenthesis to the common or default output, usually to a browser. Let's use the echo() function in a simple PHP program written to display its output in a browser window.

```
<html>
<?php echo("<h1>Greeting Earthling!</h1>" ); ?>
</html>
```

Enter this code using your text editor and then display in your favorite browser.

1. Using Server2Go, create a sub-directory in the htdocs folder and name it demo.
2. Create a text document in the demo folder named demophp. (Figure 2.1.1)

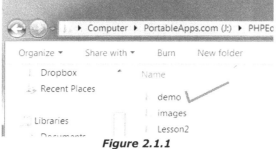

Figure 2.1.1

   3. Enter the following program in the demophp.txt file.
```
<html>
<?php echo("<h1>Greeting Earthling!</h1>"); ?>
</html>
```

4. Save As demophp.php (I use Notepad++ to do this).
   1. Open demophp.txt in Notepad++
   2. Choose Save As
   3. Select the PHP extension and save
5. Start Server2Go
6. Navigate to the demo Folder (See figure 2.1.2)

Figure 2.1.2

7. Double click on demophp.php
8. You should see a screen like Figure 2.1.3

Figure 2.1.3

If you view the source code in a browser (use View > Source) you will see:

Figure 2.1.4

```
<html><h1>Greeting Earthling!</h1></html>
```

Comments are an important part of every programming language. They are used to put documentation inside your program. This is used to help others understand your code or help you understand what you were doing when you need to maintain or reuse your code. You can do a single line comment by using the # character. All characters that follow the # character will be ignored by the compiler until the end of the line. You may also use the // (slash slash) characters and they will do the same thing.

If you need to create a comment longer than one line you may either precede each line with a # or begin the comment with a /* and end it with a */. Use comments liberally in your code. Enough to make clear what you are doing but not too much to obstruct finding the code.

PHP has approximately 70 reserved words. Reserved words are part of the syntax of the language. Words like: echo(), do, case, else, or, var, and, TRUE, FALSE, if, include(), NULL, and other reserved words must not be used for any identifier. (Appendix D)

The backslash character (\) is considered the "Escape Character". The escape character followed by a letter controls the movement of the cursor, inclusion of quotes within quotes or generation of special characters. The combination of \n causes the cursor to move to a new line. The combination of \t generates a tab character. (Appendix C)

```
<html><head><title>Escape Characters</title></head><body>
<?php
echo("<textarea rows=\"3\" cols=\"40\">");
echo ("\"The Quick Brown Fox");
echo ("\n\tJumped Over The White Fence\"");
echo ("</textarea>");
?>
</body></html>
```

Figure 2.1.1

Lesson 2.2 - Variables

A variable is an area of memory that the program uses to store data or intermediate steps of a calculation. These areas of memory are assigned names by the programmer so they can be easily referenced when needed. The rules for making up the names are as follows:
- All variables must begin with a $.
- The $ must be followed by a letter or an underscore (_).
- Variable names can only contain, letters, digits and the underscore.
- May not be a reserved word.
- May NOT contain SPACES.

Some examples of valid variable names are:
- $xyz
- $pay_rate
- $counter55

To place data in a variable, you use the assignment operator (=) as follows:

```
$pay_rate = 10.00;
$hours = 40;
$pay11 = $hours * $pay_rate;
$counter55 = $counter55 + 1;
```

16

The first two examples move an amount into the variable. The third example stores the result of multiplying $hours by $pay_rate. The fourth example adds a 1 to the contents of $counter55 and stores the result back into $counter55. We will discuss more when we study PHP arithmetic statements.

Lesson 2.3 - Strings

String data is an important concept of PHP in generating dynamic web pages. We saw a simple example in the first lesson where we used the echo() function to display a simple message. This sample program displays the Preamble to the United States Constitution in your favorite browser:

```
<html>
<?php
/* First we declare a variable named $msg.  Then we assign the string as we would
in a HTML document.  The string includes HTML code as well as the text of the
Preamble."*/
$msg = "<textarea rows=\"8\" cols=\"50\">We the people of the United States in
order to form a more perfect union, establish justice, insure domestic tranquility,
and secure the blessings of liberty to ourselves and our posterity, do ordain and
establish this Constitution for the United States of America. \n \t\t\tPreamble to
the U.S. Constitution </textarea>";
# Now display the contents of the variable $msg with the echo() function
echo( $msg );
?>
</html>
```

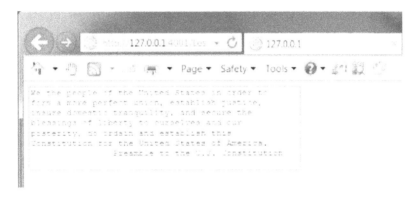

Figure 2.3.1

Note the use of comments and escape characters used to build the contents of the $msg string variable that formats the message into a textarea. The text area will hold a specified amount of data in the text box and adds a vertical scroll bar to view any text that does not fit in the box.

Lesson 2.4 - Data Types

The variables we declare in a PHP program may hold any type of data. PHP is referred to as a "loosely" typed language, a language where a variable can hold any type of data. Many other languages require that you state what type of data you will store in a variable and will give you an error if the program attempts to store data of a different type.

17

The types of data that can be stored in a PHP variable are:
- Integer - whole numbers without decimal places.
- Floating-Point - numbers with decimal places.
- Strings - groups of letters, numbers, symbols, spaces within double quotes (" ") or single quotes (' ').
- Boolean - a truth value, case insensitive using PHP keywords, TRUE or FALSE.
- NULL - a variable set to NULL has no value at all.

Example code that demonstrates using variables:

```php
<html>
<?php
    $hrs = 40;
    $rate = 9.50;
    $name = "Tim Doe";
    $gross = NULL;
    $bonus = FALSE;
    echo("Hours worked: $hrs <br />");
    echo("Rate of Pay: $rate <br />");
    echo("Employee Name: $name <br />");
    echo("Gross Pay: $gross <br />");
    echo("Bonus: $bonus <br />");
?>
</html>
```

Figure 2.4.1

Lesson 2.5 - Arithmetic Operators

We often see the computer as a giant calculator. While it is more than just a calculator, arithmetic is an important function in programming. The truth is, the computer does calculations very well. A bit of trivia is that the computer performs all arithmetic operations with addition. If you study binary arithmetic, you will see how the computer adds, subtracts, multiplies and divides using only addition.

There are eight arithmetic operators available in PHP:

Operator	Arithmetic Function
+	Addition
-	Subtraction
*	Multiplication
/	Division
%	Modulus
.	String Concatenation
++	Increment
--	Decrement

Other languages allow the + symbol to concatenate strings, PHP uses the (.) operator for string concatenation and is the only operator that can be used for this purpose. The ++ operator increments a variable by one and the -- operator decrements the variable by one.

The addition, subtraction, multiplication, and division operators are the same as we learned in grammar school. The modulus operator (%) may be new to some. It is used to perform the division operation on two integers (numbers without a decimal portion) and return only the remainder. It can be used to determine if a number is odd or even. If any number % 2, if the result is 0 (zero) the number is even, if the result is greater than 0 the number is odd.

SYNTAX:

        operand3 = operand1 + operand2

An operand may be a variable, numeric literal or calculation. The statement above reads, the value represented by operand1 is added to the value represented by operand2 and the result is stored in the variable named operand3.

Examples of the use of each of the arithmetic operators:

```
$addnum = 8.5 + 15.2;
$addstr = "John". " Q ". "Public";
$sub = 54 - 9.5;
$mult = 64 * 2;
$div = 32 / 2;
$mod = 55 % 2;
$incr = 4; $incr = ++$incr;
$decr =11; $decr = --$decr;
```

Most of the examples should be self explanatory but the last two may be a problem. The variables $incr and $decr are assigned a value. Then the second instruction increments (or decrements) the contents of the variable by one and stores the result back in the original variable. At the end $incr should contain the value 5 and the $decr should contain the value 10.

Lesson 2.6 - Assignment Operators

PHP programs may assign values to variables. Often these assignments are the result of arithmetic operations. If the variable receiving the new value is also part of the expression, assignment operators are a convenient shortcut.

There are seven assignment operators:

Equivalent	Operator	Example
$a = $b	(=)	$a = $b
$a = $a + $b	+=	$a += $b
$a = $a . $b	.=	$a .= $b
$a = $a - $b	-=	$a -= $b
$a = $a * $b	*=	$a *= $b
$a = *a / $b	/=	$a /= $b
$a = $a % $b	%=	$a %= $b

If the contents of the variable $a is 10 and the contents of the variable $b is 5 the example of the += operator in the statement $a += $b would take the value stored in $a which is 10 and add it to the value stored in $b which is 5, resulting in the value 15 which would be stored back in the variable $a. At the end of this operation, $a would contain 15 and the variable $b would contain 5.

```
<html>
<?php
    $hrs = 40;
    $rate = 9.50;
    $fname = "Tim ";
    $lname = " Doe";
    $ytd = 800.0;
    $pay = $hrs * $rate;
    $ytd += $pay;
    $fname .= $lname;
    echo($fname <br />);
    echo("YTD PAY: $ytd);
?>
</html>
```

Figure 2.6.1

20

The example program declares and initializes several variables. Then multiplies the contents of $hrs by the contents of $pay and stores the result in the variable $pay. Then the $ytd contains a number and we add to that number the contents of $pay. The next line concatenates the contents of $fname with the contents of $lname, storing the new string in $fname. The last two statements display the results.

Lesson 2.7 - Summary

There are several ways to represent a php script. The preferred way is <?php –phpcode – ?>, simple and easy to understand. Of the three types this one clearly defines the php code and is the most compact. The important part is that you select one of these types and use it consistently in all instances in all your programs.

Variables are places for the program to store the data it is working with. Variables can hold any type of data as PHP does not tie a specific data type to a variable. PHP is not a strongly typed language. Variables are always preceded by a $ (dollar sign).

While the computer is more than a calculator, arithmetic operations are an important part of any program. PHP features eight arithmetic operators. Assignment operators in PHP make some arithmetic operations simpler to code and understand.

In Review:
1. A common form for a PHP script is:
    a. <?php   php code ?>
    b. <? php code ?>
    c. <script language="php"> php code </script>
    d. all of the above
2. The PHP statements terminator is:
    a.   : (colon)
    b.   ; (semi-colon)
    c.   . (period)
    d.   // (double slash)
3. Comments are used to put documentation inside your program.
    a.   True
    b.   False
4. The escape character is:
    a.   //
    b.   #
    c.   \
    d. $
5. A _____ is an area of memory that programs use to store data.
    a.   store
    b.   save
    c.   variable
    d.   counter
6. A variable MAY NOT contain:
    a. $
    b.   numbers
    c.   upper case letters
    d.   spaces

7. To place a value in a variable, use the:
    a.   %
    b.   =
    c.   +
    d.   _
8. The variables we declare may hold any type of data.
    a.   True
    b.   False
9. There are _____ arithmetic operators in PHP.
    a.   12
    b.   10
    c.   8
    d.   6
10. The modulus operator (%) divides two numbers and returns the:
    a.   remainder
    b.   product
    c.   quotient
    d.   result

Start Programming with PHP

An Introduction to PHP and MySQL

LESSON 3: Functions

Lesson 3.1 - Overview of Functions

A function is a block of code that can be executed once or multiple times by a PHP script. PHP scripts are generally a group of variables and functions. Functions are reusable code. Write and test the code for a task once, then every time you need to perform that task in a program, call that function. This can save programming time, upload time, and testing time.

We have already used a function that is built into PHP, the echo() function. You will also find several other built-in functions as you learn more about PHP.

New functions may also be created by using the function keyword in a declaration, followed by a space, then the name you wish to give the new function, followed by a set of parenthesis. Then the code for the function enclosed in a set of curly braces {}.

```
FUNCTION SYNTAX:
          function functionname()
          {
                   function statements;
          }
```

```
FUNCTION CALL SYNTAX:
          functionname()
```

EXAMPLE of a Function:

```
<html><head><title>Function Example</title></head>
<body>
<?php   function greet() {
        echo("Welcome to PHP Functions"); } ?>
<?php greet();  ?>
<p>This is HTML code. </p>
<hr />
<?php greet();  ?>
</body> </html>
```

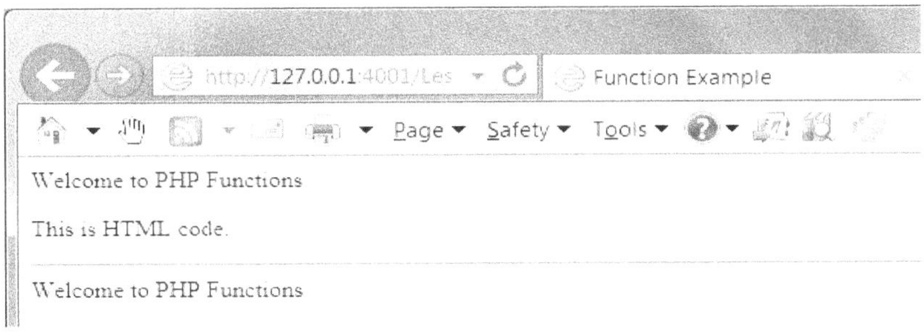

Figure 3.1.1

This function is declared in the body section of the web page. Then it is called by the second PHP script. This is followed by a paragraph stored in HTML and a solid line. Then the function is called a second time.

Lesson 3.2 - Function Arguments

The set of parenthesis that follows each function name may be empty or contain data to be passed to the function code. The data indicated in the parenthesis are referred to as arguments or parameters, these terms are used interchangeably. The function determines what arguments are required and in the order will be expected. The function call must supply those arguments in the correct data type and in the proper order.

FUNCTION SYNTAX:
```
        function functionname(argument1, argument2, .... ) {
                function statements;
        }
```
FUNCTION CALL SYNTAX:
```
        functionname(argument1, argument2, ....)
```

Using the greet() function we wrote in the last lesson, the following code illustrates the use of arguments to pass information to the argument.

Example of a function with arguments:

```
<html><head><title>Arguments Example</title></head>
<body>
<?php    function greet($txt) {
        echo("<h2>$txt</h2>"); } ?>
<p>First Greet Matthew.</p>
<?php greet("Matthew"); ?>
<hr />
<p>Next Greet Michael.</p>
<?php greet("Michael"); ?>
</body> </html>
```

Figure 3.2.1

The function greet() accepts one argument. The data passed to the function will be stored in a variable named $txt and available to all statements in the function. The first call passes a name to the function and the function displays that name in the browser. Then a horizontal line is displayed followed by a second name passed to the function by the second function call.

Lesson 3.3 – Functions that Return a Value

A function can be used to do an operation and at the end, pass a value back to the function call. The function call must then be prepared to use the return value by including it in a calculation, storing it in a variable or outputting it to a file or display. The function returns a value using the **return** statement.

```
<html><head><title>Return a Value Example</title></head>
<body>
<?php    function rtrnval($no1, $no2) {
        $total = $no1 + $no2;
        return $total;
}
$store_total = rtrnval(22, 55);
echo "Value returned from function: $store_total"
?> </body> </html>
```

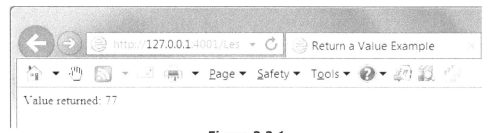

Figure 3.3.1

This will return "`Value returned from function:  77`" to the display.

The return statement only returns a single value. If it is necessary to return more than one value an array may be used.

Note the function call assigns the returned value to a variable named $store_total. The value returned must be stored in a variable, used in a calculation or displayed.

We will return the values of two numbers added, subtracted, and multiplied.

```
<html><head><title>Return a Value Example</title></head>
<body>
$num array();
<?php    function rtrnarray($no1, $no2) {
        $tadd = $no1 + $no2;
        $tsub = $no2 - $no1;
        $tmul = $no1 * $no2;
        return array($tadd, $tsub, $tmul);
}
$num = rtrnarray(22, 55);
echo "Value returned from adding: $num[0]"
echo "Value returned from subtraction: $num[1]"
echo "Value returned from multiplication: $num[2]"
```

```
?> </body> </html>
```

This will return:
```
    Value returned from adding: 77
    Value returned from subtraction: 33
    Value returned from multiplication: 1210
```
to the display.

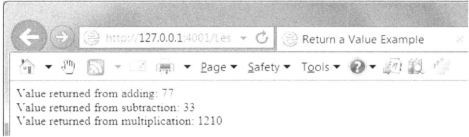

Figure 3.3.2

Lesson 3.4 – Functions and Pass Arguments by Reference

To this point we have passed values or copies of the contents of variables to functions. PHP will also allow a function to work directly with the values in the variables passed rather than just a copy of the value. This is called Passing Arguments by Reference. Passing by reference allows the function to directly alter the contents of variables declared in another PHP script or function.

```
<html><head><title>Return a Value Example</title></head>
<body>
$num array();
<?php
function passref(&$arg)
{
        $arg = 88;
}
$mynum = 11;
echo "Value Before Function Executes: $mynum"
passref(&$mynum);
echo "Value After Function Executes: $mynum"
?> </body> </html>
```

This will return:
```
    Value Before Function Executes: 11
    Value After Function Executes: 88
```
to the display.

Figure 3.4.1

Note the difference in the arguments for pass by reference. The argument to be passed by reference is preceded by a (&) ampersand. This indicates that a pointer to the variable in the calling program is to be passed to the function.

Lesson 3.5 - More About Functions

The next question is, "How many functions can I use?". The short answer is, "As many as you need.". Multiple functions may be called individually from a script or a function can call another function.

The following is an example of a program that has two functions.

```
<? php  function bytwo($num)  {
     $result = $num * 2;
     echo("The answer is: $result"); }

     function byfour($num)  {
     $result = $num * 4;
     echo("The answer is: $result");  } ?>

<html><head><title>Function I</title></head>
<body>
<p>Multiply the given number by two.</p>
     <?php bytwo(6); ?>
<p>Multiply the given number by four.</p>
     <?php byfour(6); ?>
</body></html>
```

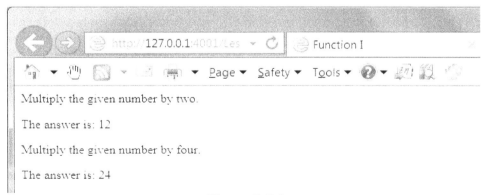

Figure 3.5.1

The two functions bytwo() and byfour() are declared. Then, in the HTML document there are two

PHP scripts, the first calls the function named bytwo() with an argument value of six (6) and the second one calls the function named byfour() with an argument value of six (6). The function calculates the answer and displays it to the browser window.

Now, let's look at a function that calls a second function.

```
<? php  function bytwo($num)  {
      $result = $num * 2;
      writeout($result"); }

      function writeout($arg)  {
      echo("The answer is: $arg");  } ?>
```

```
<html><head><title>Function II</title></head>
<body>
<p>Multiply the given number by two.</p>
      <?php bytwo(8); ?>
</body></html>
```

Figure 3.5.2

First, two functions bytwo() and writeout() are declared. Then the HTML program has a script that calls the function bytwo() with an argument value of 8. The function bytwo() performs the calculation and then calls the function writeout() passing the value calculated for printing by that function.

Lesson 3.6 - Variables with Multiple Arguments

Up to this point we have only used one argument for each function. Let's look at an example where we pass more than one argument and if the program does not supply data for an argument, a standard value (we will use 8) will be substituted for the missing data.

```
<?php  function addit($x=8, $y=8, $z=8)  {
      $result = $x + $y + $z;
      echo("The answer is: $result");  } ?>
<html><head><title>Multiple Arguments</title></head>
<body>
<p>Add 3 numbers 3, 6, and 9 and show the answer.</p>
      <?php addit(3, 6, 9): ?>
<p>Add two numbers 2, 4 and do not supply a third argument.</p>
      <?php addit(2, 4); ?>
</body></html>
```

28

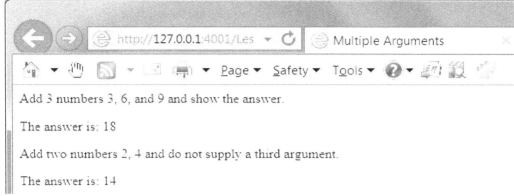

Add 3 numbers 3, 6, and 9 and show the answer.

The answer is: 18

Add two numbers 2, 4 and do not supply a third argument.

The answer is: 14

Figure 3.6.1

The function addit() is looking for 3 values. In the HTML the first call to addit supplies 3 values and should result in a value of 18 posted as an answer (3 + 6 + 9 = 18). On examination of the function addit() it not only asks for 3 arguments but gives a value to to each argument, the value 8. When we call the function with only two values (2 and 4), the value 14 is posted as the answer. This results from adding the values of 2 and 4 for the variables $x and $y plus the default value 8 for variable $z. So, 2 + 4 + 9 gives us 14 as an answer.

Lesson 3.7 - Scope of Variables

The last topic in functions is to go over the concept of the scope of variables. Scope refers to how long the contents of a variable are available to the function itself or to other functions or scripts. Understanding the scope of variables is key to learning how to pass information between functions and scripts.

The variables we have used this far have been "local" variables. This means that contents of the variable are available only to the function in which they were declared and cease to exist once the function has been exited.

If the contents of a variable is to be available to other functions and scripts, the variable needs to be declared outside of any function or script. Then when the variable is used the programmer must precede the name of the variable with the keyword "global". If the keyword global is not used it will simply declare a local variable of that name.

The following is an example of how to use global variables.

```php
<?php $ans
    function bytwo($num)  {
          global $ans;
          $ans = $num * 2;
          writeout();  }

    function writeout()  {
          global $ans;
          echo("The answer is: $ans"); }  ?>

<html><head><title>Scope</title></head>
<body>
<h2>
```

```
            <?php bytwo(16); ?>
    </h2>
    </body></html>
```

The result:

Figure 3.7.1

Note the function writeout() has no argument expected or passed to it. The function gets the value to display from the global variable named $ans.

Lesson 3.8 - Summary

A function is a block of code that the program can use repeatedly, rather than code the same task multiple times. This will make the web page more compact and hopefully, easier to understand.

Information is passed to the function in arguments. An argument consists of variables, numbers or strings. This is information passed from the calling instruction to the function. Often the function returns a value to the calling instruction. A function may have multiple arguments. Variables declared in a function only exist as long as that function is executing. As soon as the function completes, the variable and its contents no longer exist.

In Review:

1. A _____ is a block of code that can be executed once or multiple times by a PHP script.
    a.   subscript
    b.   function
    c.   segment
    d.   multi-processor
2. The set of parenthesis that follow each function name may
    a.   be empty
    b.   contain arguments
    c.   both a and b
    d.   none of the above
3. A function returns a value using the _____ statement.
    a.   send
    b.   return
    c.   break
    d.   continue
4. If a function is to return more than one value it
    a.   must use an array
    b.   cannot return more than one value.
    c.   it must contain subroutines
    d.   it must contain sub functions

5. Passing values by _____ allows the function to directly alter the contents of a variable in another PHP script or function.
   a.   value
   b.   reference
   c.   argument
   d.   parameter
6. A function may only have one argument.
   a.   True
   b.   False
7. _____ refers to how long the contents of a variable are available.
   a.   Reference
   b.   Global
   c.   Local
   d.   Scope
8. _____ variables cease to exist after the function has been exited.
   a.   Global
   b.   Local
   c.   Numeric
   d.   String
9. A variable declared outside a function is a _____ variable.
   a.   Global
   b.   Local
   c.   Numeric
   d.   String
10. When a Global variable is used, the programmer must precede the name of the variable with:
   a.   a %
   b.   a$
   c.   the key word "global"
   d.   nothing is required

Start Programming with PHP

An Introduction to PHP and MySQL

LESSON 4: Decisions

Lesson 4.1 - Overview of Decision Processing

Programs often evaluate data to make decisions in processing. If the data meets established criteria it executes one set of instructions, if it does not it executes a different set of instructions. The key to decision processing is establishing Boolean Value expressions that make the proper decisions. A Boolean Value expression is an expression that evaluates to either TRUE or FALSE. An example expression is (8 > 4) or (eight is greater than 4). This statement can only be TRUE or FALSE. Either 8 is greater than 4 or it is NOT greater than 4.

The greater than sign (>) is one of six "Relational Operators". We will review each of these in the next lesson.

Lesson 4.2 - Relational Operators

There are six Relational or Comparison Operators.

Operator	Comparison
==	Equality
!=	Inequality
>	Greater Than
<	Less Than
>=	Greater Than or Equal To
<=	Less Than or Equal To

These are used to compare two values which may also be called operands. An operand may be either a literal value or the contents of a variable.

Equality - If the number stored in the variable $num1 equal to 8, would be written ($num1==8) and if the contents of $num1 is equal to 8 the expression tests TRUE and if $num1 contains any other value the expression tests FALSE.

Inequality - If the value stored in the variable $response not equal to 'Y' would be written ($response !='Y') and if the contents of $response is equal to any value other than 'Y' the expression tests TRUE and if the value in $response is a 'Y' the expression test FALSE.

Greater Than - If the number stored in the variable $ans is greater than the value stored in the variable $count the expression would be written as ($ans > $count). If the contents of $ans are larger than the contents of the variable $count the expression is TRUE. If the contents of $ans is NOT greater than the contents of the variable $count the expression tests FALSE. So, if $ans contains 4 and $count contains 4 the expression tests FALSE because 4 is NOT greater than 4.

Less Than - If the number stored in the variable $ans is less than the value stored in the variable $count the expression would be written as ($ans < $count). If the contents of $ans are smaller than the contents of the variable $count the expression is TRUE. If the contents of $ans is NOT less than the contents of the variable $count the expression tests FALSE. So, if $ans contains 4 and $count contains 4 the expression tests FALSE because 4 is equal to 4 NOT less than 4.

Greater Than or Equal To - If the test is to find if a number in one variable is greater than or equal to the number in another variable the expression would be written as ($a >= $b). So, if $a contains 5 and $b contains 3 the expression evaluates to TRUE because 5 is greater than 3. If $a contains 5 and $b contains 5 the expression still evaluates to TRUE because 5 is equal to 5.

Less Than or Equal To - If the test is to find if a number in one variable is less than or equal to the number in another variable the expression would be written as ($a <= $b). So, if $a contains 2 and $b contains 3 the expression evaluates to TRUE because 2 is less than 3. If $a contains 5 and $b contains 5 the expression still evaluates to TRUE because 5 is equal to 5.

Some additional examples where $a = 10 and $b = 5:

Expression	Evaluates To
$a > $b	TRUE
$a < $b	FALSE
$a != $b	TRUE
$b >= $a	FALSE
$b <= $a	FALSE
$b >= 5	TRUE
$a > 11	FALSE
$5 == 5	TRUE

The comparison of the two values ALWAYS results in a TRUE or a FALSE. These are known as Boolean Expressions.

Lesson 4.3 - Decision: If Statement

The PHP If statement evaluates an expression for a Boolean Value (TRUE or FALSE). If the expression evaluates to TRUE it executes a single statement or a statement block (more than one statement enclosed in curly braces { }).

An example of code that evaluates an expression and if TRUE executes a single line of code. If the expression evaluates to FALSE the statement after the TRUE statement is executed.

```
<html><head><title>Conditional IF</title></head>
<body>
        <?php $age = 18;
        if($age >= 18) echo("You may vote");
        echo("End of Program");  ?>
</body></html>
```

33

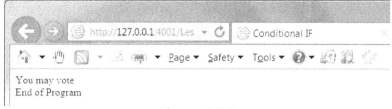

Figure 4.3.1

Now, lets change the contents of the variable $age to a number lower than 18 and rerun.

An example of code that evaluates an expression and if TRUE executes a statement block.

```
<html><head><title>Conditional IF</title></head>
<body>
      <?php $age = 10;
      if($age >= 18) {
            $msg = "You are  eligible to vote";
            echo($msg);
            }
      echo("End of Program");  ?>
</body></html>
```

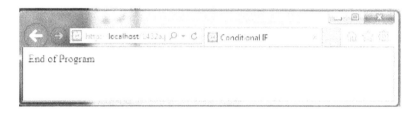

Figure 4.3.2

Again, experiment with this program using values greater than 18 and less than 18.

Lesson 4.4 - Decision: If ... Else Statement

In the cases where an expression is evaluated and it is necessary to do one set of code when the Boolean Value is TRUE and a different set of code when the Boolean Value is FALSE, we use the If...Else statement.

To construct the If ... Else statement, add the else keyword after the code to be executed when the expression evaluates to TRUE and then follow the else keyword with the statement block or statement to be executed when the Boolean Value is FALSE.

Example of If ... Else Statement.

```
<html><head><title>If Else Statement</title></head>
<body>
      <?php $age= 8;
      if ($age >= 18)
            {
```

```
                    $msg = "You are eligible to vote";
                    echo($msg);
                    }
            else
                    {
                    $msg = "You are too young to vote";
                    echo($msg);
                    }
            echo("End of Program");
            ?>
    </body></html>
```

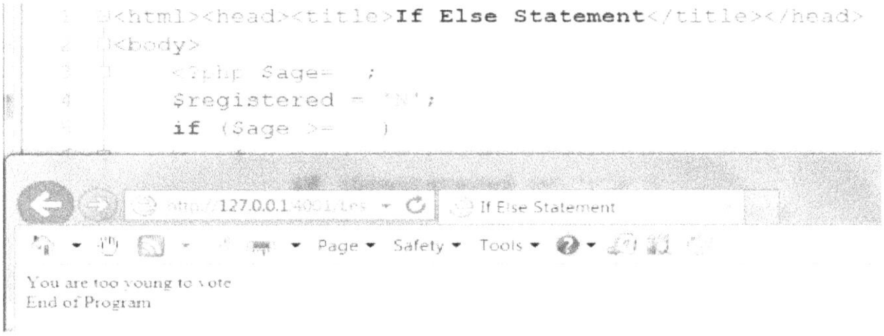

Figure 4.4.1

The example declares a variable named $age and initializes it to 8. The If statement then tests the expression to determine if it is greater than or equal to 18. If the result is the Boolean Value True it does the statement block immediately following the line with the If statement. Then continues with the statement "echo("End of Program")". If the result of the expression is the Boolean Value FALSE, the program skips to the Else keyword and executes the code immediately following that line. Then continues with the statement "echo("End of Program")".

Lesson 4.5 - Decision: Nested If Statements

Often it is necessary to code an If statement within other if statements when more comparisons are necessary to complete the processing. This is referred to as a "nested if" statement. This can be coded in a single sided if statement or on the true or false sides of an If ... Else statement.

Let's look at a simple example of the nesting of an if statement.

```
    <html><head><title>If Else Statement</title></head>
    <body>
            <?php $age= 28;
            $registered = 'Y';
            if ($age >= 18)
                    {
                            If ($registered == 'Y') {
                            $msg = "You are eligible to vote";
                            echo($msg);
                            }
                    else
                            {
```

35

```
                    echo("You need to register to vote")
                    }
        else
            {
            $msg = "You are too young to vote";
            echo($msg);
            }
        echo("End of Program");
        ?>
  </body></html>
```

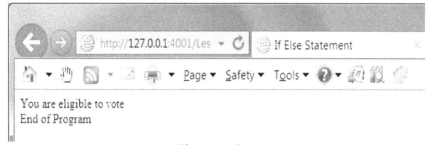

Figure 4.5.1

In the example $age is set to 28 and $registered is set to 'Y'. The rule is that you need to be 18 or older and registered to vote. If you are under 18 you may not vote nor could you be registered. The first or outer if statement tests to see if the person is old enough to vote and if TRUE then the nested loop tests to see if the person is registered and if TRUE allows the user to vote or if not registered (tests to FALSE) reminds the person they need to be registered to vote.

If $age is initialized to 28 and $registered is initialized to N, the resulting output would look like this:

```
1  <html><head><title>If Else Statement</title></head>
2  <body>
3      <?php $age=    ;
4      $registered = 'N';
5      if ($age >=   )
6          {
7              if ($registered ==  'Y')  {
```

You need to register to vote
End of Program

Figure 4.5.2

The first test on $age evaluates to true but the second evaluation of $registered evaluates to false resulting in the message "You need to register to vote".

The number of nests of if statements is undefined, but should be restricted to three or four nests. After that, the program becomes hard to read and understand. If more nests are required there is another decision structure called the Switch statement that is easier to use and understand. (See Lesson 4.7).

36

Lesson 4.6 - If ... Else in a Function

If statements may also be used in functions. We discussed functions in the last chapter and know that a function can contain any valid PHP statements. So, it is entirely possible we will find If statements in functions or use them in functions we write.

Testing to find out if a number is odd or even is will be required in several places in an application to be written. So, a function that does this task will have to be written. This example will be a function that takes one argument and tests to see if the value in that argument is odd or even.

```
<? php  function oddeven($num)  {
        $result = $num % 2;
        if ($result == 0)  {
                echo("The number is EVEN.");
        else
                echo("The number is ODD.");  } ?>

<html><head><title>Function I</title></head>
<body>
<p>Pass an even number to the function:</p>
        <?php oddeven(6); ?>
<hr />
<p>Pass an odd number to the function:</p>
        <?php oddeven(7); ?>
</body></html>
```

Figure 4.6.1

The HTML code in the example tests the function first with an even number and then with an odd number.

Lesson 4.7 - Decision: Switch Statement

An effective alternative to nesting a bunch of If ... Else statements is the Switch statement. It can be used to check a variable for a number of different values or ranges of values. It is easier to understand than the if statements nested and can be more efficient when there are a large number of possibilities to be tested.

Our example will look at the contents of a variable that may contain values from 1 to 5 and display the text for that number.

```
<html><head><title>Switch Statement</title></head>
<body>
<?php
        $num = 3;
        switch($num)
        {
                case 1 : echo("One"); break;
                case 2 : echo("Two"); break;
                case 3 : echo("Three"); break;
                case 4 : echo("Four"); break;
                case 5 : echo("Five"); break;
                default : echo("Invalid Entry");
        }
        echo("The Program Terminates");
?>
</body></html>
```

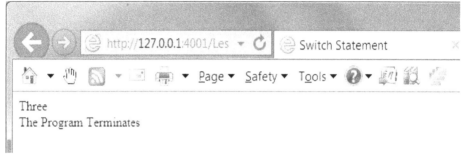

Figure 4.7.1

The example switch statement examines the contents of the variable $num which, by definition must be an integer from 1 to 5. Any other value will be declared invalid. When the contents of $num is a 1 the program will display the text "One". The echo() function is followed by a break statement. The purpose of the break statement is to exit the statement block and continue with the statement following the end of the statement block, in this case a message indicating the program has terminated. The program compares for values 1 to 5 and provides an echo() function and a break statement that are executed if the comparison is TRUE. If the value is not found there is a default statement that displays an "Invalid Entry" message indicating a valid value was not found.

If certain values are more likely to be selected than other values, placing the more popular selections first may result in faster execution times.

Lesson 4.8 - Summary

An important part of a programming language is the decision structure. The ability to examine data and decide which of two possible alternatives will process the information correctly. These decisions are based on evaluation using one of six relational operators. These operators are used to compare two values (also called operands) and return a boolean result (True or False).

The decision statements are the single sided *if* statement, the *if...else* statement (two-sided), and the *switch* statement. The single sided *if* statement evaluates an expression and if it evaluates to true the statement or statements in the following code block are executed. If the expression evaluates to false the processing continues at the next valid instruction.

The *if...else* evaluates an expression and if true does the first statement block after the *if* statement. If false the statement block after the *else* keyword.

The *switch* statement is used when a variable is used to indicate several choices. Based on the value contained in the variable, different code is executed.

In Review:

1. There are ____ relational operators.
    a.   2
    b.   6
    c.   8
    d.   11
2. Relational operators are used to compare two values called _____
    a.   operands
    b.   parameters
    c.   globals
    d.   locals
3. The comparison of two values always results in:
    a.   True or False
    b.   a higher number
    c.   a lower number
    d.   program crash
4. In cases where an expression is evaluated and it is necessary to do one set of instructions if the expression is true, and a different set of instructions if false.
    a.   If...Then..Endif
    b.   If...Or
    c.   If...Else
    d.   Select..Or
5. If statements encoded within other If statements are referred to as _____.
    a.   stacked
    b.   nested
    c.   global
    d.   contained
6. If statements may not be used in a function.
    a.   True
    b.   False
7. An alternative to using several nested If statements is the _____ statement.
    a.   group
    b.   select
    c.   switch
    d.   none of the above
8. Each Case statement in a Switch statement is ended with a _____ statement.
    a.   continue
    b.   go
    c.   stop
    d.   break

Start Programming with PHP

An Introduction to PHP and MySQL

LESSON 5: Repetition

Lesson 5.1 - Overview of Repetition (or Looping)

Making decisions is an important part of programming. Equally important is the repetition or looping structure. The ability to repeat sequences of programming statements, makes programs very powerful. Imagine doing a payroll and it is necessary to run the program start to finish for each employee. This might work for a company with just a few employees but would be onerous for large companies with hundreds or thousands of employees. So, the ability to run the program repeatedly without user intervention is very important.

Repetition is used to process files of data, arrays, games, as a matter of fact, most applications require, at some point, the repetition structure. It may be to run the entire program repeatedly or just a segment of the code. It is not uncommon for a program to include many repetition structures.

We will examine several types of loops. The simplest is the FOR loop and this is a loop used when the number of repetitions is known or can be calculated as the program is running. Then the more complex pretest loops and post test loops. These loops are performed until some condition exists. The desired relationship between two operands is reached, the end of a file is reached or a sentinel is encountered. All of these true or false conditions can be used to terminate a loop.

Pretest loops test the condition before any loop instructions are executed, therefore the instructions in the loop may never be executed if the initial condition tests false. A post test loop goes through the loop instructions at least once before testing the loop condition. Note that if code inside the loop does not change the loop condition, it produces what is referred to as an "infinite loop". That is a loop that never ends and the program looks like it freezes the computer.

Lesson 5.2 - The FOR Loop

This loop is used when the program knows, or can calculate how many times to repeat the group of instructions (loop). It specifies the start, condition that will terminate the loop, and optionally the increment value each time through the loop.

SYNTAX: for (initialize counter variable; completion expression; increment counter variable)
                    { loop statements; }

The for keyword is followed by a set of parenthesis. Inside the parenthesis is 3 components. First you must declare and initialize a counter variable. Next is a boolean expression that compares the counter variable to a ending value. Last is the value to increment or decrement the counter variable at the end of each loop iteration. If the number is positive the counter variable is incremented and if negative the counter variable is decremented. The starting value of the counter variable must be larger than the ending value if incrementing the counter.

```
<html><head><title>For Loop </title></head><body>
     <?php
          for($index = 1; $index <= 10; $index += 1)  {
               echo $index;
```

```
     } ?>
</body></html>
```

Figure 5.2.1

In this example the variable $index is initialized to one. The variable $index is compared to the value 10 and the loop continues as long as the value of $index is less than or equal to 10. Each time the loop completes the value in $index is incremented by 1. Once the value in $index is greater than 10 the loop exits to the next instruction following the end of the loop instructions which are contained in a set of curly braces {}.

```
<html><head><title>For Loop </title></head><body>
     <?php
          for($index = 10; $index <= 0; $index -= 1) {
               echo $index;
     } ?>
```

In this example the variable $index is initialized to ten. The variable $index is compared to the value 0 and the loop continues as long as the value of $index is greater than 0. Each time the loop completes the value in $index is decremented by 1. Once the value in $index is equal to 0 the loop exits to the next instruction following the end of the loop instructions which are contained in a set of curly braces {}.

Lesson 5.3 - The FOREACH Loop

The foreach loop is specifically used for arrays and objects.

```
     <?php
          foreach($myarray as $value) {
               echo $value;
     } ?>
```

See Lesson 6 on Arrays for further explanation.

Lesson 5.4 - Pretest Loops (while)

The while loop is a pretest loop. This means that before any of the instructions in the loop are executed a Boolean condition must test false. To enter the loop the condition is tested and must evaluate to true, according to the relational and/or logical operators used for the loop instructions to be executed. The pretest loop may or may not execute the loop statements. This is because the boolean condition is tested before the loop instructions are executed, if it tests false, the loop is ended and exits the loop structure. If the boolean condition tests to true the loop instructions are executed. An instruction within the loop instructions must change the boolean condition so that it eventually tests false. If the condition never tests false the programmer has created what

41

is called an "infinite loop".

The syntax for the while loop is:

```
while (condition)
        {
                loop statements
        }
```

While the condition tests true the loop statements execute. As soon as the condition tests false, the statement after the closing curly brace will be executed.

EXAMPLE:

```
<html><head><title>For Loop </title></head><body>
<?php
        $index = 0;
        while ($index <= 10)  {
                $index += 1;
                echo $index;
        }   ?>
</body></html>
```

Figure 5.4.1

Note the output starts with 1 and goes to 11. This is due to the placement of the increment instruction in the loop where $index is incremented by one BEFORE the contents of $index is displayed.

Lesson 5.5 - Post test Loops (do...while)

The do...while loop structure sees the least use of any of the other repetition structures. It is a post test loop which means that the instructions in the loop will be executed at least one time depending on the Boolean expression in the while clause at the end evaluates to true or false.

SYNTAX

```
        do
                {
                        loop statements;
                }
        while(boolean expression);
```

The do keyword marks the beginning of the loop. The statements enclosed in the curly braces {} are the loop statements. The while(boolean expression) is tested after the closing curley brace. If true, processing returns to the do statement, if false, processing continues to the next

42

instruction after the while statement. As with any loop, one of the loop statements must change the condition tested at the beginning of the loop so that, at some point, the condition will test false and the loop will be exited. If a loop is constructed so that there is no way out of the loop it is called an "infinite loop".

EXAMPLE:

```
<html><head>
<title>Post Test Loop</title>
</head><body>
      <?php
            $index = 0;
            do  {
                  $index += 1;
                  echo $index;
            }  while ($index <= 10);
      ?>
</body></html>
```

Figure 5.5.1

The value of $index is set to zero and then the program begins the loop. The first instruction adds one to the value in $index, the second instruction displays the contents of $index. The while clause compares the contents of $index and as long as the value is less than or equal to ten the loop continues. Once the value printed is eleven (11), the loop condition tests false and the loop exits.

This is an example of an instance where the loop executes only once:

```
<html><head>
<title>Post Test Loop</title>
</head><body>
      <?php
            $index = 10;
            do  {
                  $index += 1;
                  echo $index;
            }  while ($index <= 10);
      ?>
</body></html>
```

43

Figure 5.5.2

The value of $index is set to ten and then the program begins the loop. The first instruction adds one to the value in $index, the second instruction displays the contents of $index. The while clause compares the contents of $index and since the value of $index is now eleven (11) the while clause tests false and the program exits.

Lesson 5.6 - Nested Loops

When one loop is placed inside another loop the structure is referred to as a nested loop. We can place any code structure inside a loop including another loop structure. Loops in Loops, decisions in loops, loops in decisions, decisions in decisions. These are a common occurrence in programs.

To place a while loop within another while loop, the syntax would look like this:

```
while (condition)
    {
    statements;
    while (condition)
        {
        statements;
        }
    statements;
    }
```

A sample application using nested loops:

```
<html><head>
<title>Nested Loop</title>
</head><body>
<?php
    $a = 0;   $b=5;   $c=10;   $sum1=0; $sum2=0;
    while($a<5)
        {
        $a++;   $sum1++;
        echo("Start Outer loop $a <br />");
        while($b>0)
            {
            $b--;   $sum2++;
            echo("Inner Loop $b <br />");
                }
    $b = 5;
        echo("Finish Outer Loop $a <br />");
        }
    echo ("<br />Outer Sum = $sum1,  Inner Sum = $sum2");
?>
</body></html>
```

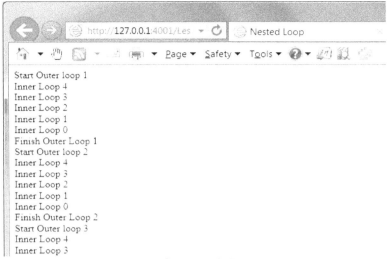

Figure 5.6.1

Lesson 5.7 – Interrupting Loops

There are instances where a condition exists that the program may have to exit the loop before a condition is met or when the loop statements may be interrupted and the program flow needs to be returned to the start of the loop

The break statement is used to terminate a loop prematurely. When a break statement is encountered, control is passed to the statement after the end of the loop.

The syntax for the break statement is:

```
break;
```

EXAMPLE – break
```
do {
    if ($age >= 18)
        echo("You are old enough to vote.");
    else
        break;
    if ($registered == 'Y'
        echo("Go ahead and vote");
    else
        echo("You need to register to vote.");
    $count++;
while ($count < 10);
```

The loop first examines the contents of $age and if it is equal to or greater than 18 the program prints "You are old enough to vote." and the next if statement is executed. If the contents of $age are less than 18, the else clause executes which contains a break statement. This causes the program to exit the loop at the instruction following the statement "while($count < 10);".

The continue statement is used to pass control back to the start of the loop without completing the remainder of the statements in the loop.

The syntax for the continue statement is:

45

```
                    continue;

EXAMPLE – continue
        $count = 0;
        while ($count < 10)  {
            $count++;
            if ($count == 5)
                {  echo("Continue executed at: "$count);
                    continue;  }
            echo($count);
        }
```

The loop examines the variable $count and if the value is less than ten, the loop statements execute. The variable $count is incremented by one and then examined. If the value in $count is equal to five (5), the message "Continue executed at: 5" and control is passed back to the beginning of the loop. The statement echo($count); is not executed. The next time through the loop, the count is resumed normally.

Lesson 5.8 - Summary

The Repetition Structure or Looping adds real power to the programming language. The ability to execute a block of code repeatedly is powerful. Used to process files, arrays, multiple data submissions are all tasks that are facilitated by the repetition structure.

We looked at four basic looping or repetition structures: FOR, FOREACH, WHILE, and DO...WHILE loops. The first three are pretest loops and the fourth is a post test loop. The pretest loop examines the loop condition prior to doing the loop instructions. If the expression evaluates to true the loop instructions are executed and program flow returns to the beginning at the evaluation statement. If the expression evaluates to false the loop is not executed and flow is directed to the next instruction after the loop.

In a post test loop, the loop evaluation expression is at the end of the loop instructions. The expression is evaluated after the loop instructions have been executed once. Then the expression is evaluated and if true, control is returned to the beginning of the loop instructions. If false the next instruction will be executed.

In Review:

1. The repetition structure is also known aw the _____ structure.
        a.   continue
        b.   looping
        c.   repeat
        d.   redo
2. The best loop to use when the number of loops is known or can be calculated, is the _____ loop.
        a.   while
        b.   dowhile
        c.   for
        d.   switch

3. Which is not a component of the for loop that is enclosed in parenthesis
   a. initialize a counter variable
   b. a boolean expression that compares the counter variable to an ending value
   c. a value used to increment or decrement the counter variable at the end of the loop
   d. all of the above
4. The _____ loop is specifically used for arrays and objects
   a. pretest
   b. posttest
   c. foreach
   d. while
5. A _____ loop may never execute any of the loop instructions.
   a. pretest
   b. posttest
   c. foreach
   d. while
6. A _____ loop executes the loop instructions at least one time.
   a. pretest
   b. posttest
   c. foreach
   d. while
7. The _____ loop is an example of a pretest loop.
   a. do...while
   b. switch
   c. foreach
   d. while
8. The _____ loop is an example of a posttest loop
   a. for
   b. do..while
   c. foreach
   d. while
9. When a loop is placed inside another loop, the structure is referred to as a _____ loop.
   a. pretest
   b. posttest
   c. stacked
   d. nested

An Introduction to PHP and MySQL

LESSON 6: Arrays

Lesson 6.1 - Overview of Arrays

An array is similar to a variable. By definition a variable can only contain a single value. An array is simply a variable that can hold multiple values. Each value is an element of the array and each element has a reference number called the index. To refer to a specific element, you use the array name plus the index number of the element enclosed in square brackets [].

Before we get started with arrays there are some rules for naming arrays.
- Names must begin with a dollar sign.
- The dollar sign may be followed by either a letter or an underscore
- Complete the name with any combination of digits, letters, or the underscore.

Arrays automatically begin with an index number of zero (0) unless otherwise indicated. We will discuss this further in a later lesson.

Lesson 6.2 - Creating Arrays

To define an array you use the array() function. The syntax for array declaration is:

```
array();
        or
array("Mon", "Tue", "Wed");
        or
array(5, 6.7, 8.90, 10, 4, 13.85, 16);
```

The first example defines an array of an undetermined size. The second is an array of three string variables. The last is an array of seven numeric values.

We will declare an array and the load the array with 4 numeric values.

```
<?php
        $myArray();
        $myArray[0] = 123;
        $myArray[1] = 456;
        $myArray[2] = 789;
        $myArray[3] = 555;
?>
```

First we declare an array called $myArray of an undetermined size. Then we load the first element of that array with the value 123. Note how we address the first value, $myArray[0]. The index number for the first element of the array is zero (0). Arrays are zero based. This means that the first element is 0 and the second, is 1, etc.. Even though there are four elements the highest index will be three (3). This may take some practice to get used to this numbering scheme but with some practice it will come together.

Lesson 6.3 - Using Arrays

The programmer can write code to add elements to an array, update elements in an array and delete elements from an array.

In PHP the array can contain data of different types within the same array. Each array element has its own index value starting with zero (0). The combination of the array name and the index value, direct the program to the correct element in the array. In the next example we will declare an array initialized with three string values. Then we will print those values. Next, we will load the same array with three decimal values and print them. Then, the last section loads the array with a string, a decimal number, and an integer and prints those values. This demonstrates the flexibility of arrays in PHP.

```php
<html><head><title>Array Values</title></head>
<body>
      <?php
            $myArray= array("Red", "White", "Blue");
            print ($myArray[0] . " " . $myArray[1] . " " . $myArray[2]);
            $myArray[0] = 12.34;
            $myArray[1] = 23.45;
            $myArray[2] = 45.67;
            print ($myArray[0] . " " .$ myArray[1] . " " . $myArray[2]);
            $myArray[0] = "Green";
            $myArray[1] = 12.55;
            $myArray[2] = 99;
            print ($myArray[0] . " " . $myArray[1] . " " . $myArray[2]);
      ?>
</body></html>
```

Figure 6.3.1

In this example you have seen that we can initialize an array to values at the time we declare the array, Change the values (update) the array values within the program, updating the elements without regard to the constraints of a data type.

To add an element to an array lets examine the following code:

```php
<html><head><title>Array Values</title></head>
<body>
      <?php
            $emp= array();
            $emp[0] = 6789;
            $emp[1] = "Jon Doe";
            $emp[2] = 10.85;
            print ($emp[0] . " " . $emp[1] . " " . $emp[2]);
      ?>
</body></html>
```

49

Figure 6.3.2

This program declares an array of unlimited size and then adds three elements to the array. Jon Doe receives a salary increase to 12.15, we can update the array by the following command.

$emp[2] = 12.15;

This statement addresses the element of the array $emp with the index number of 2 and replaces the contents of this element which is 10.85 to the new value, 12.15.

Deleting elements or entire arrays will be covered in Lesson 6.5.

Lesson 6.4 – Listing Array Elements

PHP makes looping though an array easy with the foreach function. Use the AS keyword to point to the element as you step through the loop. The syntax of the foreach function is:

```
foreach($array AS $key => $value)
        { current $key and $value; }
```

Consider an array named $emp containing the names of all employees in the company. The key is their index number and the value is their name.

```
<html><head><title>Listing Arrays</title></head>
<body>
<?php
        $emp = array("Doe", "Gray", "Moore", "Files", "Jones", "Simms");
        $key = 0;
        foreach($emp AS $key => $emp)
                {
                        print "$key: $emp<br />";
                }
?>
</body></html>
```

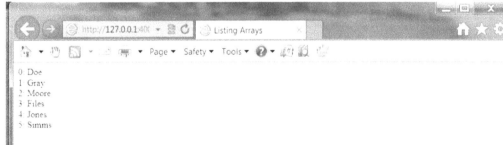

Figure 6.4.1

This simple program will list the index number, a colon and the employee name, one per line in the browser window.

50

Lesson 6.5 - Array Functions

There are several functions that are useful in processing arrays. The first is a function that allows the program to get the number of elements in an array. As a matter of fact, there are two such functions that do the same job. The first is count() and the other is sizeof(). We will use count() for our examples but they both work exactly the same.

```
$elements = count($newarray);
echo("Total number of elements in the array: $elements")
```

These two statements get the number of elements in the array named $newarray, store in a variable named $elements, and then display a message revealing how many elements were found.

A second useful function is one to delete an element of an array or if necessary delete the entire array.

```
unset($array[2]);
```

Deletes the array element with the index number 2.

```
unset($array);
```

Deletes the entire array named $array.

A function named array_merge() allows you to append one array at the end of a second array.

```
$new_emp = array_merge($emp , $newhire);
```

The result here would be an array named $new_emp that would contain the contents of the array named $emp followed by the contents of the array named $newhire.

If necessary an array can be sorted. You can sort the values in ascending sequence sort() or in descending sequence using rsort().

The shuffle() functions randomly reorganizes the order of the specified array.

Lesson 6.6 - More about Arrays

In all of my examples I have used the index to an array as a number. PHP allows more flexibility in this area than does many other programming languages. In the first lesson we established that the index of the array began with zero and used this concept for our examples to this point. However there is more flexibility in the PHP programming language.

Consider one of our earlier examples:

```
<html><head><title>Listing Arrays</title></head>
<body>
<?php
        $emp = array("Doe", "Gray", "Moore", "Files", "Jones", "Simms");
        $key = 0;
        foreach($emp AS $key => $emp)
```

```
                    {
                        print "$key: $emp<br />";
                    }
        ?>
        </body></html>
```

Figure 6.6.1

If we wanted the key to be used as an employee number, we could set up our array as follows:
$emp(21=>"Doe", 22=>"Gray", 23=>"Moore", 24=>"Files", 26=>"Jones", 30=>"Simms");

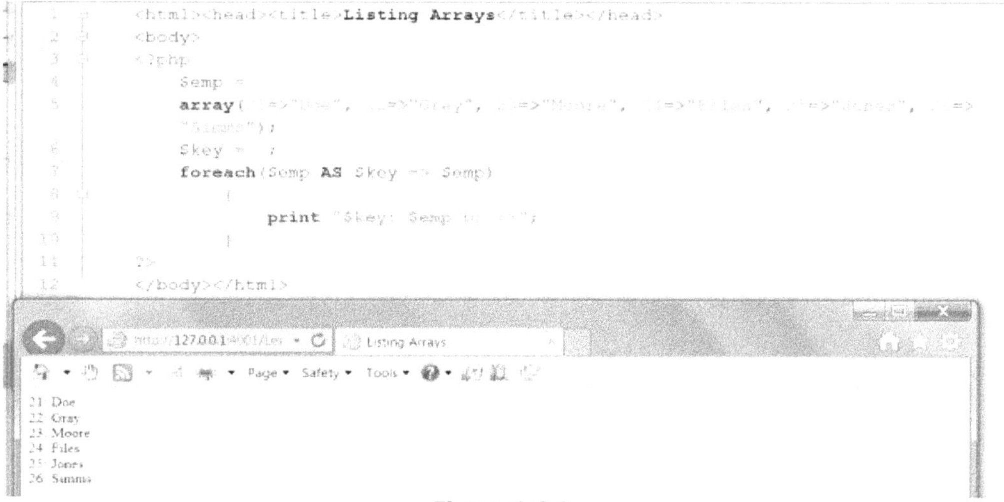

Figure 6.6.2

Now the index to the array $emp would be their employee number.

It gets even better. We can build an array of Class Numbers and Class Names:

```
$class = array(
        'CMP104' => 'Intro to Computer Programming',
        'CMP107' => 'Windows Operations',
        'CMP115' => 'Fundamentals of Computer Architecture',
        'CMP117' => 'Visual Programming'
        );
```

52

Figure 6.6.3

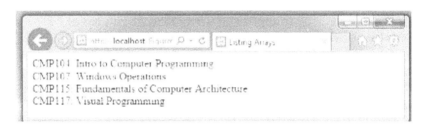

Figure 6.6.4

The pointer to each element of the array is the course number and the array element contains the course name. Think about the possibilities here.

Lesson 6.7 - Summary

An array is a variable that can store multiple values. A good example is an array that holds the names of the days of the week. All seven day names would be held in this variable. They would be referenced by using the variable (array) name plus a subscript (a number in parenthesis). The first value in the array is: arrayname + (0) subscript zero.

The FOREACH repetition structure is ideal for writing and reading data to and from an array.

Array processing is made easier by the inclusion of several built-in functions, standard in PHP. The count, unset, array_merge, resort and shuffle are just a few of the functions designed to simplify array processing.

In Review:

1. An array is similar to a _____.
    a.   statement
    b.   variable
    c.   object
    d.   operand

2. The index number of an array is enclosed in:
   - a.   [ ]
   - b.   { }
   - c.   ( )
   - d.   < >
3. Arrays automatically begin with an index number of ____ unless otherwise indicated.
   - a.   1
   - b.   one
   - c.   0
   - d.   null
4. The statement array(); creates
   - a.   an array of undetermined size
   - b.   an error message
   - c.   a message to the user to input the array size at run time
   - d.   none of the above
5. The programmer can write code to:
   - a.   add elements to an array
   - b.   update elements in an array
   - c.   delete elements from an array
   - d.   all of the above
6. The instruction to declare an array with 3 values is:
   - a.   array[3];
   - b.   array{3};
   - c.   array(3);
   - d.   array<3>;
7. PHP makes looping through an array easy with the _____ loop.
   - a.   while
   - b.   do..while
   - c.   foreach
   - d.   switch
8. There are two functions that allow the program to get the number of elements in an array.
   - a.   count(), size()
   - b.   nbr(), size()
   - c.   count(), nbr()
   - d.   count(), sizeof()
9. Use _____ to delete an entire array.
   - a.   unset();
   - b.   delete(all);
   - c.   delete();
   - d.   unset(all);

Start Programming with PHP

An Introduction to PHP and MySQL

LESSON 7: PHP, the Internet, and Email

Lesson 7.1 - Browsers

Different browsers display PHP differently. Even different versions of browsers may have some effect on how the PHP generated page renders on the display. This is a good reason for testing your PHP programs in different browsers and different versions of the browsers. As your web site runs it is a good idea to monitor the site statistics for the different browsers used to access your site and optimize it for the browser and version most often accessing your site.

Some of the more popular browser that you should consider are:
- Firefox
- Chrome
- Internet Explorer
- Safari
- Opera

Remember, if you optimize for only the current version of a browser, you may be penalizing a large percentage of viewers who are working with older equipment and software. If you are trying to attract the techies, by all means, optimize for the latest technology. If you are marketing to the senior citizen crowd, you may want to look good in a wide cross section of older browsers.

PHP comes with a number of helpful environment variables. You can see a list of these variables by looking at the output of the function phpinfo(). It will also provide browser details by using the getenv() function. The following example shows how to display the browser information.

```
<html>
<head><title>GETENV Function</title></head><body>
<?php      $browserenv = getenv("HTTP_USER_AGENT");
           echo("Browser Information:<br />$browserenv");
?>
</body></html>
```

Figure 7.1.1

These variables can help your program identify the browser and version of the browser that will view the page that the program will be composing. This can be used to customize the page to offer the best experience for the viewer.

Lesson 7.2 - Servers

When considering the environment for your web site, it is important to consider both the browser and the server. Often the server is not considered and some subtle problems are encountered when moving from one server platform to another. In considering the server we need to look at the operating system and the software that serves up the web pages. We will look at the two most popular operating systems and the two most popular software products.

The two most popular operating systems are:

Windows: Windows Server is the Microsoft entry into operating systems used to run web server application software. Internet Information Server (IIS) software is the Microsoft application software that is designed to work with the Windows operating system to serve web pages. Note that Windows may also use the Open Source Apache Web Server software.

Linux: The Linux operating system comes in many versions. Many versions have server configurations to run web servers. It is important to note that the Microsoft Windows IIS does NOT run on the Linux operating system.

The two most popular web server software products are:

Internet Information Server (IIS): IIS runs only on the Microsoft Windows Operating System. It is the second most popular web server software. When writing your web pages you do not need to worry about case for your internal web site links. IIS is NOT case sensitive.

Apache: Apache is the most popular web server software. It is used by just over fifty percent of the web servers on the internet today. When writing pages to be served by Apache, it is important to note that you must realize that it considers case when resolving internal web site links.

There are other less popular web servers that are such a small percentage of the servers used that we will not discuss them here. However, all of the web server software works so much alike, other that the one instance noted above, that unless you look for some differences they all work the same.

Lesson 7.3 - Form Actions

PHP is a great tool for handling the data submitted by the user to the server when using HTML forms. Each field submitted from an HTML form sends the data as key-value pairs. The key is the input name and the value is the content of the field.

There are two methods of transmitting form data from the browser to the server. If you look in the form element in the example below, it has a method argument. The method argument can be either GET or POST. Each method has its own benefits and you need to choose the most appropriate method based on the features of the method.

GET - This method handles requests where the response page will never change. It is the simplest type of method and is used for the simple retrieval of static HTML documents, images, or the result of a database query. The get method is the default method if no method is specified in the form element. Form data is sent via the URL and is limited to less than 1240 bytes including the URL information.

POST - Used when the processing of the form modifies a database, updates a shopping cart, or sends an email message. The data is bundled in an HTTP message body and is more secure than the get method. It can also handle larger amounts of data.

The action property of the form element indicates which php script will handle the data at the server side. It must show the name of the php program with the extension as well as any path information required.

An example of a simple HTML form that asks the user for their name, their favorite operating system and the name of their favorite programming language:

```
<html><title>Form Example</title></head><body>
<form action="prog.php" method="post">
<strong>Enter your first name:</strong>
<input type="text" size="20" name="progname"> <br />
<strong>Select your favorite operating system:</strong>
<input type="radio" name="os" value="Windows"> Windows
<input type="radio" name="os" value="Linux"> Linux
<input type="radio" name="os" value="MacOS"> MacOS <br />
<strong>Enter your favorite programming language:</strong>
<input type="text" size="20" name="proglang"> <br />
<input type="submit" value="Send Form">
</form>
</body></html>
```

Figure 7.3.1

In the <form> tag, the action attribute points to a file named "prog.php". This indicates the PHP program that will process this data. It may display the information back to the browser, store the data in a file or database or both. Our example will look at the data and display it back on the browser screen:

```
<html><title>Form Data Submitted</title></head><body>
<?php
if ($progname != null)
      {echo("Thank you $progname<br />"); }
if (($os != null) and ($proglang != null))
      {echo("You program in $proglang<br />");
      echo("on the $os Operating System<br />"); }
?>
</body></html>
```

Figure 7.3.2

57

This will display the information submitted in your browser window.

Lesson 7.4 - Data Manipulation

Some forms on websites are designed to accept data from the form, manipulate the data and return a result from the data manipulation. It may be something as simple as taking a few numbers, performing a calculation, and return a result to the browser. It may take information from the form, store the information in a file, get additional information from a database, perform a calculation and finally return information to the browser.

We will look at an example that asks the user for the length of a rectangle, the width of a rectangle and then allow the user to determine if the perimeter or the area of the rectangle will be calculated.

```
<html><title>Calculation Example</title></head><body>
<form action="cal.php" method="post">
<strong>Enter the width of the rectangle:</strong>
<input type="text" size="20" name="width"> <br />
<strong>Enter the length of the rectangle:</strong>
<input type="text" size="20" name="length"> <br />
<strong>Select the calculation:</strong>
<input type="radio" name="calc" value="Perimeter"> Perimeter
<input type="radio" name="calc" value="Area"> Area <br />
<input type="submit" value="Calculate">
</form>
</body></html>
```

Figure 7.4.1

At the server the program "cal.php" would look like this.

```
<html><title>Rectangle Information</title></head><body>
<?php
if (is_numeric($width) && is_numeric($length))
    {if ($calc != null)
    { switch($calc)  {
        case 'Perimeter' : $ans = ($width + $length) * 2; break;
        case 'Area' : $ans = $width * $length); break;
        }
    echo("The answer is: $ans")}
else { echo("Non Numeric Entry found"); } }
?>
</body></html>
```

Figure 7.4.2

Once the program has determined that it has two numeric values using the is_numeric() function, it uses the switch statement to evaluate the choice of radio button and does the appropriate calculation.

Lesson 7.5 - PHP Email

A PHP program can generate a form that sends an email to a specific email address. Plain text emails or HTML formatted email messages may be sent. Emails may be sent with attachments.

As with any form data PHP should validate the generated email to prevent incomplete forms from being submitted.

Lesson 7.6 - Sending Email

Before you can send emails from PHP, some changes must be made to the php.ini file so the mail() function can find the appropriate mail server.

The PHP language is available for Windows, Linux, Unix, and Mac OS. There are many different versions of each operating system, so the customization of the php.ini file can vary. The best way for you to make your changes is to look up the configuration for your particular version of your operating system is to look it up on Google. This is the best way to make sure you get the proper values for the appropriate properties in the file.

The email related properties of the php.ini file are:
- STMP (Simple Mail Transfer Protocol) - The main email property that specifies the server that will accept and deliver messages from a PHP program. The default location is localhost but can be configured to point to your local ISP's mail server.
- smtp_port - The default value is port 25. This is the assigned port for sending and receiving email.
- sendmail_from - Empty by default. It is used to specify the default "From" value for your messages.
- sendmail_path - Used to set the path to the local sendmail program.

The mail() function is the PHP function that generates and sends the email as directed by the configuration of properties in the php.ini file.

SYNTAX:
```
mail(to, subject, message[, additional headers[, additional parameters]]);
```

The values may be strings or variables containing strings.

to:	recipient of message
subject:	subject of message
message:	the actual message
additional_headers:	optional, header information usually for HTML
additional_parameters:	depends on mail server and version of server

59

EXAMPLE:

```
    mail(you@yoursite.com, "Recent Order", "Thank you for your recent order.",
"From: me@mysite.com");
```

To test out the email we need to create a user feedback form that we will confirm with a text confirmation email and an HTML confirmation email. Our simple feedback form:

```
    <html><head><title>Order Feedback Form</title></head>
    <body>
        <form action="feedback.php" method="post">
        Name:<input type="text" name="username" size="50" />
        <br /><br />
        Email:<input type="text"name="useradd" size="50" />
        <br /><br />
        <textarea name="comments" cols="50" rows="10" >
        </textarea><br />
        <input type="submit" value="Send" />
        </form>
    </body></html>
```

PHP can send plain text emails and HTML emails.

```
    <?php
    $recipient = "you@yoursite.com";
    $msgSubject = "Recent Order";
    $msgContent = "Thank you for your recent order.";

    mail($recipient, $msgSubject, $msgContent);
    ?>

    <html><head><title>Confirmation</title></head><body>
    <h2>Thanks for your order</h2>
    Confirmation received from <?php echo($username); ?> <br />
    Reply to <?php echo($useradd); ?>
    </body></html>
```

Send as HTML email:

```
    <?php
    $recipient = "you@yoursite.com";
    $msgSubject = "Recent Order";
    $msgContent = "Thank you for your recent order.";
    # set content type header for HTML mail
    $msgHead = "MIME-Version: 1.0\r\n";
    $msgHead .= "Content-type: text/html; ";
    $msgHead .= "charset=iso-8859-1\r\n";
    $msgHead ,= "From: me@mysite.com \r\n";
    $msgHead .= "CC: boss@bosssite.com \r\n";
```

```
mail($recipient, $msgSubject, $msgContent, $msgHead);
?>

<html><head><title>Confirmation</title></head><body>
<h2>Thanks for your order</h2>
Confirmation received from <?php echo($username); ?> <br />
Reply to <?php echo($useradd); ?>
</body></html>
```

Lesson 7.7 - Error Checking

In our examples above there is no error checking. In an actual form application, each field must be checked to insure the user has entered appropriate data in the fields requested. You will note on many web forms there is a note at the top that indicates that all fields marked with an asterisk (*), usually in red, must be completed. This indicates that those fields will be checked to insure there is valid data in each of those fields. Email addresses must also be validated to insure that they are in a valid email format. The code for error checking the email address in our example in the last lesson using the preg_match() function, may look like this:

```
if( !$useradd )
{ $errmsg .="Email Address Required <br />";
      $valid = false; }
else
{ $useradd = trim($useradd);
  $_name = "/^[-!#$%&\'*+\\/0-9=?A-Z^_`{|}~]+";
  $_host = "([-0-9A-Z]+\.)+";
  $_tlds = "([0-9A-Z]){2,4}$/i";
  if (preg_match($_name."@".$_host .$_tlde,$useradd) )
  {$errmsg .="Email address has incorrect format! <br />;
    $valid = false; }
}
```

Other fields in the form are much less complicated to validate.

Lesson 7.8 - Summary

Operating Systems, Browsers, Servers all dictate the users online experience. The PHP programmer must recognize these differences and write code that insures that these differences do not adversely affect the user's online experience.

We gather information from users on the internet using forms. The data returned to the server from these forms is where PHP shines. PHP can manipulate this data, retrieve data from databases, write data to databases, write data to files, send new information back to the user plus a myriad of other tasks.

We can use PHP to generate emails to users based on requests, information entered in forms or even to all of the customers on a database. Yes, even generate spam!

61

In Review:

1. A good reason for testing your PHP program in several different browsers and in different versions of browsers is:
   a.   to insure each browser accepts code from PHP.
   b.   different browsers may display PHP generated code differently
   c.   different browsers require different PHP statements
   d.   none of the above

2. PHP programs can see a list of helpful environment variables with the _____ function.
   a.   environment();
   b.   getenviron();
   c.   phpinfo();
   d.   phpenviron();

3. PHP can get browser details from the _____ function.
   a.   browser();
   b.   browseinfo();
   c.   getbrowser();
   d.   getenv();

4. _____ runs only on a Microsoft Server.
   a.   IIS
   b.   Apache
   c.   WebServ
   d.   TomCat

5. _____ is used by over 50% of all web servers.
   a.   IIS
   b.   Apache
   c.   WebServ
   d.   TomCat

6. There are two methods of transmitting form data from the browser to the server.
   a.   GET, PUT
   b.   SEND, GET
   c.   GET, POST
   d.   PUT, POST

7. The _____ method transmits form data via the URL and is limited to 1240 bytes including the URL information.
   a.   SEND
   b.   PUT
   c.   POST
   d.   GET

8. Data sent from a form should always be _____.
   a.   validated
   b.   scanned
   c.   deleted
   d.   numeric

9. Before you can send emails from PHP, some changes must be made to the _____ file
   a.   email.ini
   b.   browser.ini
   c.   php.ini
   d.   apachemail.ini

10. The _____ function is used to determine if a value is a numeric value.
   a.   isnumber();
   b.   notalpha();
   c.   isnum();
   d.   isnumeric();

Start Programming with PHP

An Introduction to PHP and MySQL

LESSON 8: Working with Files

Lesson 8.1 - Overview of Files
Stored data is essential to many applications. Most online applications store data in databases, but there are some applications that rely on storing data in simple text files.

Files consist of records and records consist of fields. The file is generated sequentially, one record at a time. When the data is used it is usually retrieved sequentially, one record at a time.

Text files are a common and universal way to store contact information, guestbooks, comments and other candidates for storage in a file structure other than a database. Text files are a quick, inexpensive means of storing data that will be processed at a later time. This is usually data that will have no immediate use within an application but will be processed by another application or possibly edited and later fed into a database.

Lesson 8.2 - Open and Close Files
Before attempting to open a text file you need to store the path to the file in a variable.   This allows the program to find the file or the directory where the file should be created if it does not exist. Then the file can be opened. The fopen() function opens the file pointed to by the variable containing the path to the directory containing the file or where the file should be written. The syntax of the fopen() function is:

```
$file = fopen($filenamevar, mode);
```

The mode parameter may be one of the following choices:

Mode	Purpose
r	Read Only Pointer at the beginning of the file
r+	Read and Write Pointer at the beginning of the file
w	Write Only Pointer at the beginning of the file Existing file data will be lost If file does not exist it is created
w+	Read and Write Pointer at the beginning of the file Existing file data will be lost If file does not exist it is created
a	Write Only Pointer at the end of the existing file If file does not exist it is created
a+	Read and Write Pointer at the end of the existing file If file does not exist it is created

Depending on the location of your files you may or may not need to provide a path to insure the program can find the file(s) required. The examples below, show an example where the file is in a subdirectory of the C drive. The second shows how to address a file that is in the same directory as the PHP program processing the file.

```
EXAMPLE 1:

       $fn = "C:\server2go\htdocs\textfiles\input.txt";
       $file = fopen($fn, "w");

EXAMPLE 2:

       $fn = "input.txt";
       $file = fopen($fn, "w");
```

After the program has finished processing a file, the file should be closed. It is a good practice to close files, this insures that all data gets written from the buffer to the file. This insures you will not loose data. The fclose() function closes the file. The syntax of the function is:

```
       fclose($file);
```

Lesson 8.3 - Reading Files.

Once a text file has been opened you may read, write, append to the file depending on the mode you used to open the file. To read the entire file you have opened as read only (mode r) your code might look something like this:

```
       <html><head><title>Read a Text File</title></head><body>
       <?php
             $fn = "L83.txt";
             $read_file = fopen($fn, "r");
             $size = filesize($fn);
             $data = fread( $read, $size);
             fclose($read);
             echo ( "Characters Read: $size" );
             echo ( "<pre>$data</pre> );
       ?>
       </body></html>
```

To test your program, create a text file in the same folder as your PHP program document and name the file "L83.txt":

```
       PHP PROGRAMMING:

       PHP can be used to create interactive and dynamic web sites.  You can use
       PHP with many different operating systems.  Windows, Linux and Mac OS
       all support the PHP programming language.  PHP is an easy to learn
       programming language and builds on your knowledge of HTML, helping you
       create the web sites that are both interactive and dynamic.
```

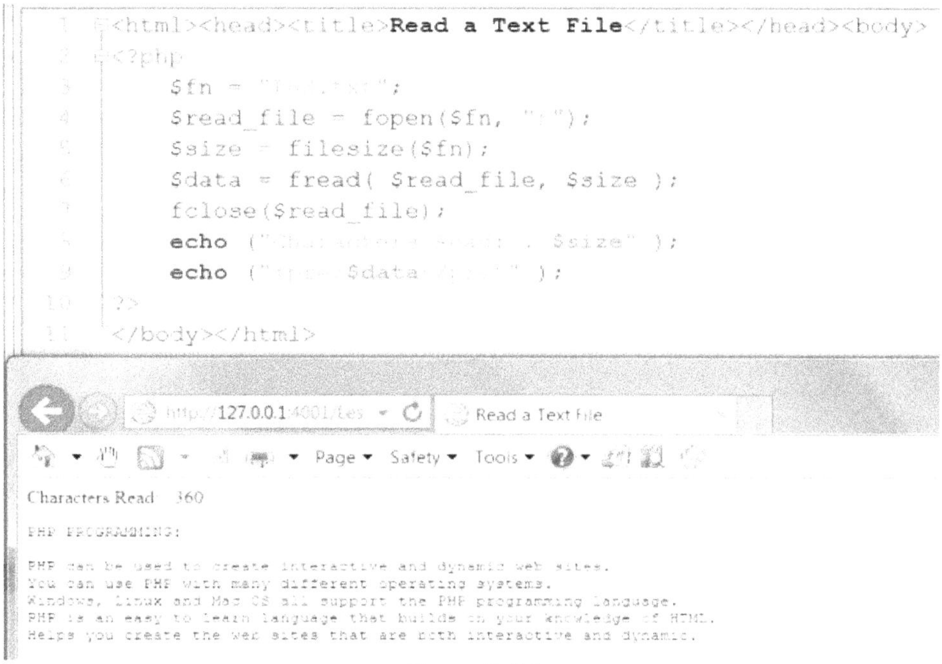

```
1    <html><head><title>Read a Text File</title></head><body>
2    <?php
3        $fn = "Test.txt";
4        $read_file = fopen($fn, "r");
5        $size = filesize($fn);
6        $data = fread( $read_file, $size );
7        fclose($read_file);
8        echo ("Characters Read : $size" );
9        echo ("<pre> $data </pre>" );
10   ?>
11   </body></html>
```

Characters Read 360

PHP PROGRAMMING:

PHP can be used to create interactive and dynamic web sites.
You can use PHP with many different operating systems.
Windows, Linux and Mac OS all support the PHP programming language.
PHP is an easy to learn language that builds on your knowledge of HTML.
Helps you create the web sites that are both interactive and dynamic.

Figure 8.3.1

There are other commands to read files from a text file. The file() function reads everything from a file and places that information into an array. Each array element consists of one line from the file which is terminated by a newline (\n) or (\r\n).

The fgets() function returns a line of text from a file. There is an optional parameter to limit the length of the line that will be read. The default is 1042 bytes of data and omitting the length parameter will read until the end of line.

EXAMPLE

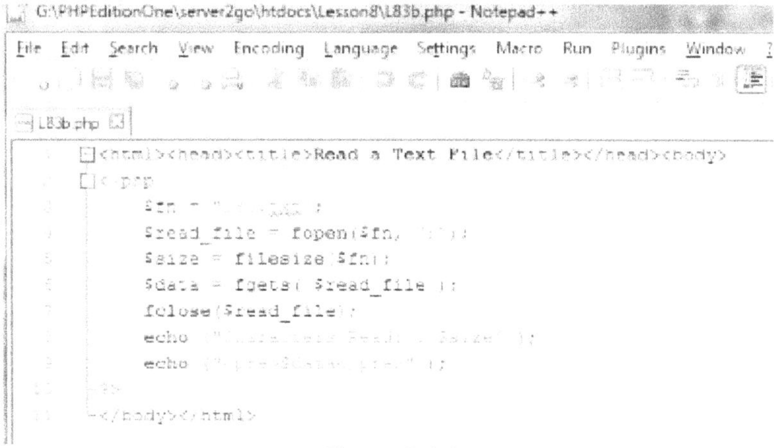

Figure 8.3.2

Figure 9.3.2 shows the program that uses the fgets() function to read the file named L83.txt, the same file we read with the fread() function. We did not include the optional size parameter and as expected, it only read up to the end of line of the first line of the text file. However, note that it did read the full 360 characters in the file.

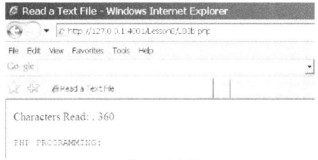

Figure 8.3.3

The fgetss() function works just like fgets() but it will strip out all HTML and PHP tags as it reads the data from the file.

Before using these statements, check with the documentation for the version of PHP that you are using. There may be some differences in versions in default values and features of the various functions.

Lesson 8.4 - Writing Files

Writing files is another set of functions available in PHP. Once the file has been successfully opened in a write mode(see Lesson 8.2), you can write to the file using the fwrite() function.

```php
<?php
    $fn = "carfile.txt";
    $outfile = fopen($fn, "w");
    fwrite($outfile, "Aston Martin amartin@hotcars.com\n");
    fclose($fn);
?>
```

Figure 8.4.1

66

In our example, the file named "carfile.txt" will be opened. The variable $fn is set to the name of the file, including extension. The file is then opened by the fopen() function using the arguments for the filename ($fn) and the file mode "w" which tells PHP to open the file for writing. The program refers to this file using the object variable named $outfile.

We can check to see if a file has been created and if created find out how many bytes of information are stored in the file. The file size information is passed in the $filesize() function.

```
<html><head><title>Write a Text File</title></head><body>
<?php
      if( file_exists( $fn ) )
      {
      $filelen = filesize($fn);
      $msg = "File : $fn ";
      $msg .= "created.  Contains $filelen bytes.";
      echo( $msg );
      }
      else { echo("File cannot be created"); }
?>
</body></html>
```

Figure 8.4.2

Next we will append a record to the end of the file we just created. For this we open with a mode of either "a" or "a+".

```
<?php
      $fn = "carfile.txt";
      $outfile = fopen($fn, "a");
      fwrite($outfile, "Lionel Trane ltrane@trains.org\n");
      fclose($fn);
?>
```

67

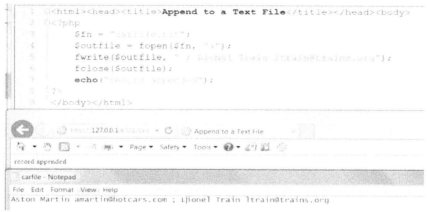

Figure 8.4.3

Now read the new file and notice the changes.

Lesson 8.5 - File Maintenance

In this lesson we will go through the maintenance procedures how to copy, rename, and delete files. These functions allow programs to do basic maintenance on files.

First we will make a copy of the file created in the last lesson (carfile.txt). The copy() function is used to make a copy of a file. This function has two parameters, the first is the original file name and the second is the new file name.

    copy(sourcefile, destinationfile);

The following program uses the copy() function to make a copy of a file on the desktop named carfile.txt, the new file is named newcar.txt:

```
<?php
$oldf = "carfile.txt";
$newf = "newcar.txt";
if (copy ($oldf, $newf) )
      { $msg = "Success: <br />Copied $oldf <br /> to $newf File."; }
else
      { $msg = "File &oldf not copied" }
?>
<html><head><title>Copy a File</title></head><body>
<?php echo($msg); ?>
</body></html>
```

68

Figure 8.5.1

Files may be renamed by using the PHP rename() function. This function takes two arguments, the original name of the file and the new name for the file. If the rename is successful, it returns a true value, if it is not successful, it returns a false value. A simple example of using the rename function is as follows:

```php
<?php
$oldf = "carfile.txt";
$newf = "vehicles.txt";
if ( rename( $oldf, $newf ) )
{ $msg = "$oldf is now $newf"; }
else
{ $msg = "Unable to rename $oldf"; }
?>
<html><head><title>Rename</title></head><body>
<?php echo($msg); ?>
</body></html>
```

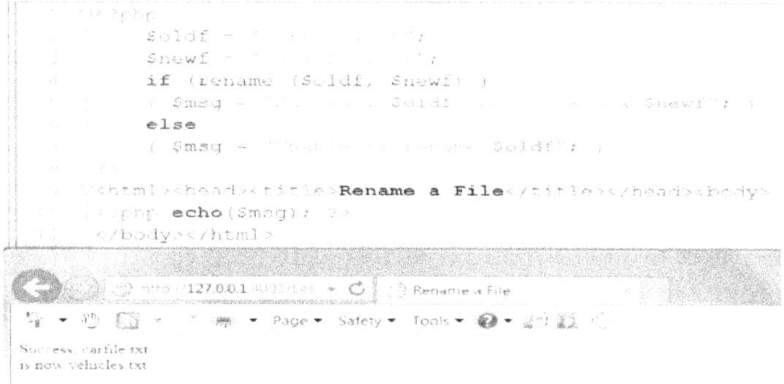

Figure 8.5.2

69

To delete a file use the PHP unlink() function. The only argument required is the name of the file to be deleted. The following code deletes the newcar.txt file.

```php
<?php  function my_delete($file)
       {
       if (unlinke($file) )
       { echo("$file<br />DELETED<hr />"); }
       else
       { echo("$file<br />NOT deleted<hr />"); }
?>
<html><head><title>Delete File</title></head><body>
<?php
       $f1 = "newcar.txt";
       $f2 = "oldcar.txt";
       my_delete($f1);
       my_delete($f2);
?>
</body></html>
```

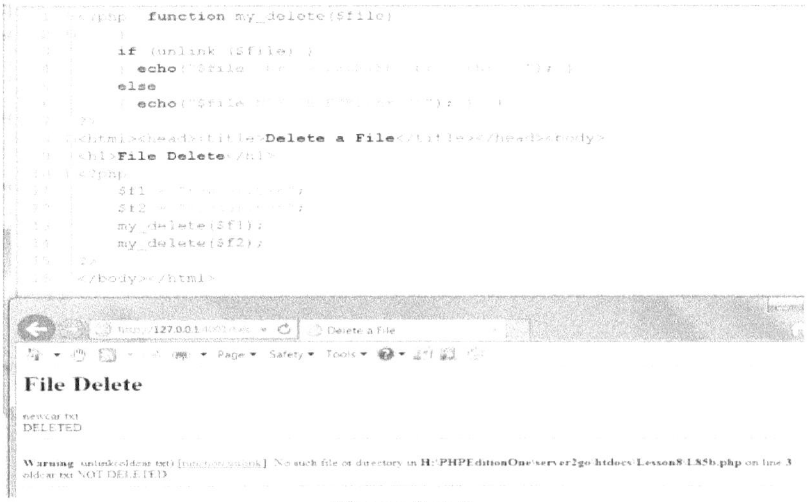

Figure 8.5.3

Note the first file should be deleted. The second file does not exist and should give an error message.

Lesson 8.6 - Saving Forms Data to Files

We gather data on forms, it is important to have the software to store this data. The data may be stored to a database, a text file or perhaps sent to an email address for further processing. It may be sent to several different destinations.

Our example will require a form that asks the user to enter and submit their name and email address. This will be transmitted via the POST method to the server where it will be processed by the php script indicated by the form element action property.

70

The HTML file:

```
<html><head><title>Request Form</title></head><body>
<h2>Request for Information</h2>
<form method="post" action="savetxt.php" >
      Name: <br />
      <input type="text" name = "user_name" size = "50" >
      <br />
      Email: <br />
      <input type="text" name = "user_email" size = "50" >
      <br />
      <br />
      <input type="submit" name = "Submit" value = "Submit" >
      </form>
</body></html>
```

The PHP script: (savetxt.php)

```
<?php
$name = $POST[ "user_name" ];
$email = $POST[ "user_email" ];
$fn = "email.txt";
      $outfile = fopen($fn, "a");
      fwrite($outfile, "Name: $name Email: $email\n");
      fclose($fn);
?>
```

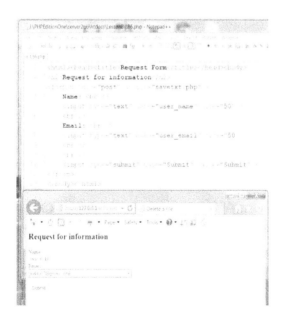

Figure 8.6.1

The HTML file should produce a file containing the name an email address entered in the HTML form. The PHP script named savetxt.php is used by the active attribute of the form tag to process

71

the data submitted. Since it was opened as an append, it will add any amount of data entered through the HTML form.

Figure 8.6.2

Lesson 8.7 - Uploading Files
A user may upload files to a server from an HTML page. Files are uploaded to a temporary directory designated in the php.ini file property upload_tmp_dir. Usually the maximum upload size is specified in the php.ini file in the upload_max_filesize property.

The following are the steps for uploading a file:
- HTML page to obtain a filename and a submit button to upload. The user provides the full path and file name and clicks on the submit button.
- File is sent to the temporary directory on the server.
- Once the entire file is received, it is then copied to the intended destination.
- PHP script confirms receipt to the user.

HTML code for the file uploader form:

```
<html><head><title>Uploader</title></head><body>
<h1>Upload Files Form </h1>
<h3>File to upload: </h3>
<form action="up.php" method="post" enctype="multipart/form-data">
      <input type="file" name="file" size="50">
      <br />
      <input type="submit" value="UPLOAD">
</form>
</body></html>
```

Next we need an upload script named up.php.

```
<?php
if ( $file_name != "" )
{
```

```
        copy("$file", "$file_name" )
        or die("Not able to copy requested file");
}
else { die("No Filename Entered"); }
?>


<html><head><title>Upload File</title></head><body>
<h2>FILE UPLOAD COMPLETED!</h2>
<ul>
        <li>SENT: <?php echo "$file_name"; ?> </li>
        <li>SIZE: <?php echo "$file_size"; ?> </li>
        <li>TYPE: <?php echo "$file_type"; ?> </li>
</ul>
<a href="<?php echo "$file_name" ?>">
        Click Here to view file</a>
</body></html>
```

If the file is uploaded successfully, the confirmation page will be received and the user will be allowed to view the file by clicking on the link provided.

Figure 8.7.1

Request the name of the file to upload, or Browse for the file.

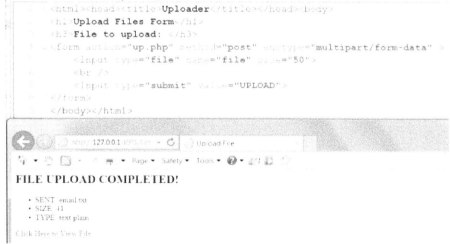

Figure 8.7.2

73

Upload complete message showing the name of the file, the size and the type of file.

Figure 8.7.3

This shows the file contents.

Lesson 8.8 - Directories

PHP has functions that may be used to display the list of files in any directory on the system. The opendir() function requires a directory handle (the drive letter and path to the directory).

The script shows both a windows solution and a linux solution. There is only one line different, the line that places the directory handle in the variable $dirname. Then it opens the directory. Next, a while loop to read the directory until it has read the entire directory. Then an if statement that skips printing the first two entries in any directory which are the "." indicating a pointer to the current directory and the ".." indicating a pointer to the parent directory. Any other filename is processed. The contents of the directory is added to the specified variable ($file_list). Any time the opendir() is used, the file should be closed when the operation is complete using the closedir() function.

The PHP script below displays the contents of the directory specified by the given directory handle.

```php
<?php
#windows code
$dirname = "C:\\DATA\\DEMO";
# the code for linux:  $dirname = "/usr/home/....";
$dir = opendir($dirname);
while ( false != ($file = readdir($dir) ) )
{
        if ( ( $file != "." ) and ( $file != ".." ) )
        {
                $file_list .= "<li>$file";
        }
}
closedir($dir)
?>

<html><head><title>List the Directories</title></head>
<body>
<p>The files in directory:
```

74

```
        <?php echo( $dirname); ?> </p>
        <ul>
                <?php echo($file_list); ?>
        </ul>
</body></html>
```

Sample output of this program:

Figure 8.8.1

Lesson 8.9 - Summary

The topic for this lesson was the handling of files. Often data gathered online is not directly placed into a database. It may be stored in a sequential file for later verification of the data or editing of the data for future entry into a database or for other uses.

When dealing with files, the first task is to open the file in the proper mode, read, write, or append the data. Then the file may be processed. PHP can read files, write files, copy files, rename files, and delete files. When file processing is complete the file should be closed.

Other tasks that may be accomplished in a PHP program is the ability to upload files from the users computer for storage on the server. PHP scripts are often used to handle this task. PHP also has the ability to examine the contents of directories and to display the directory's contents.

In Review:

1. Files consist of _____.
        a.   fields
        b.   records
        c.   numbers
        d.   directories
2. Records consist of _____.
        a.   fields
        b.   files
        c.   numbers
        d.   directories
3. Before attempting to open a text file you need to store the _____ in a variable.
        a.   USB drive
        b.   file name
        c.   disk drive
        d.   file size

4. The _____ function opens the file.
   - a.   fwrite()
   - b.   fgets()
   - c.   fopen()
   - d.   fclose()
5. The _____ function returns a line of text from a file
   - a.   fwrite()
   - b.   fgets()
   - c.   fopen()
   - d.   fclose()
6. The _____ function writes data to a file.
   - a.   fwrite()
   - b.   fgets()
   - c.   fopen()
   - d.   fclose()
7. PHP can delete a file using the _____ function.
   - a.   fwrite()
   - b.   fclose()
   - c.   fdelete()
   - d.   unlink()
8. Which open function will open a file called car.txt in a mode that will add new records to the existing file.
   - a.   `$fn = "car.txt";`
          `$outfile = fopen($fn, "a");`
   - b.   `$fn = car.txt;`
          `$outfile = fopen($fn, "a");`
   - c.   `$fn = "car.txt";`
          `$outfile = fopen($fn, a);`
   - d.   `$fn = car.txt;`
          `$outfile = fopen($fn, a);`
9. The _____ function is used to make a copy of a file.
   - a.   cut()
   - b.   duplicate()
   - c.   copy()
   - d.   clone()
10. The rename() function takes _____ arguments.
   - a.   no
   - b.   1
   - c.   2
   - d.   There is no rename() function.

76

Start Programming with PHP

An Introduction to PHP and MySQL

LESSON 9: Cookies or Sessions?

Lesson 9.1 - Overview of Cookies.

A cookie is just a text file that can be stored on the client computer. It can contain approximately 4,000 characters. A web site can place around 20 cookies on a client computer and the client computer can hold several hundred cookies.

These cookies are plain text files so often the contents are encoded to protect sensitive information. They are used to hold information like user preferences, shopping cart selections, and similar information. They are rarely used to hold sensitive information like passwords. If cookies are involved in passwords, they are generally used to hold some value that points to the password stored in a database on the web site server.

Only the program that placed the cookie on the client can use the contents of the cookie. So, the chance that another program from another site can read your data is remote. However, if the data is sensitive it should not be stored in a cookie or at least encoded to make it as difficult as possible to get the information.

Lesson 9.2 - Using Cookies.

PHP creates cookies with the setcookie() function. The function must be placed before any other code. The cookie is part of the header information and an error will occur if not properly placed.

```
<html><head><title>Invalid Cookie</title></head><body>
<?php
        setcookie("Bad", "Cookie");
?>
</body></html>
```

The correct way to set the cookie is as follows:
```
<?php
        setcookie("Good", "Cookie");
?>
<html><head><title>Valid Cookie</title></head><body>
<?php

?>
</body></html>
```

The following examples demonstrate setting cookies and reading cookies back. The first script starts by storing a name, background color and a favorite operating system in three cookies. The second script reads them and uses the data in a web page. The name is stored in a cookie called **uname**, the background color in a cookie called **ubg**, the favorite operating system in a cookie called **uos**.

FILE: setcookie.php

```php
<?php
if( ( $name != null) and ($os != null) and ($bg !=null) )
{
        setcookie ( "uname", $name, time()+2592000 );
        setcookie ( "uos", $os, time()+2592000 );
        setcookie( "ubg", $bg, time()+2592000);
        header("Location:getcookie.php" );
        exit();
}
?>


<html><head><title>Make Cookie Data</title></head><body>
<form action="<?php echo($PHP_SELF); ?>" method="post">

Please enter your first name:
<input type="text" name="name"> <br /><br />

Please enter your favorite operating system:
<input type="text" name="os"> <br /><br />

Please enter the background color for your page:
<input type="radio" name="bg" value ="#cc0000">Red
<input type="radio" name="bg" value ="#00cc00">Green
<input type="radio" name="bg" value ="#0000cc">Blue
<br /><br /> <input type="submit" value="Submit">

</form>
</body></html>
```

In the above script the form action gets the script to execute from the php system variable named **$PHP_SELF**. This directs the submit button to execute the php script at the top of the code. The screen should look like this:

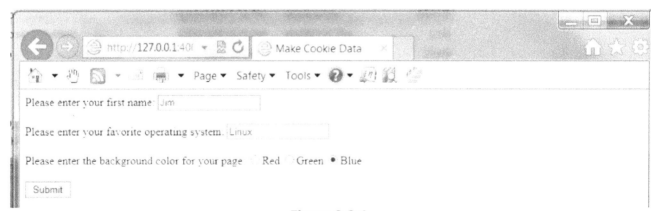

Figure 9.2.1

The next page gets information from the three cookies we set in the first HTML script. The name is in **uname,** the operating system in **uos** and the background-color in **ubg**. The data in ubg sets the background-color to the selected color and then displays the name and operating system on the web page.

78

After the setcookie.php program has run, the cookie should be set up containing the first name, the favorite operating system and the background color selected. The following program readcookie.php can then be executed to create an HTML page using the contents of the cookie as parameters.

FILE: readcookie.html

```
<html><head>
<title>Use the Cookie Data</title>
<style type="text/css">
body { color:white; background-color:<?php echo( $ubg ); ?> }
</style>
</head><body>
<h1>Hello, <?php echo( $uname ); ?>! </h1>
<br />
<h2>Your favorite operating system is: <?php echo($uos ); ?></h2>
</body>
</html>
```

Figure 9.2.2

Cookies may be used to limit access to a web page. The next example asks for a user name and password and looks at a cookie name **auth** for the correct password. If a match, the user is granted access to the page. The first page sets the cookie and the user enters both a user name and password. The browser is then redirected to a second page that checks the password. If this page finds the cookie is correct the user is redirected to a third page. If the cookie is validated, the user is allowed to view the third page.

login.php: (Figure 9.2.3)

```
<?php
if( ($uname is != null) and ($upwd != null) )
{
        setcookie("auth", "ok");
        header("Location:loggedin.php" );
        exit();
}

<html><head><title>Make Cookie Data</title></head><body>
```

79

```
<form action="<?php echo($PHP_SELF); ?>" method="post">

User Name:
<input type="text" name="user"> <br /><br />

Password:
<input type="text" name="pwd"> <br /><br />

<input type="submit" value="Login">

</form>
</body></html>
```

Figure 9.2.3

loggedin.php: (Figure 9.2.4)

```
<?php
header("Cache-Control:no-cache");
if( !$auth == "ok" )
{ header("Location:login.php" ); exit(); }
?>
<html><head><title>Logged In</title></head><body>
Login successful and you have full access to the web site <a href="mainpage.php"> Go to another
site page</a>
</body></html>
```

Figure 9.2.4

mainpage.php: (Figure 9.2.5)

```
<?php
```

80

```php
header("Cache-Control:no-cache");
if( ! $auth == "ok" )
{ header("Location:login.php" ); exit(); }
?>
<html> <head><title>Still Logged in </title></head><body>
You are still logged in
</body></html>
```

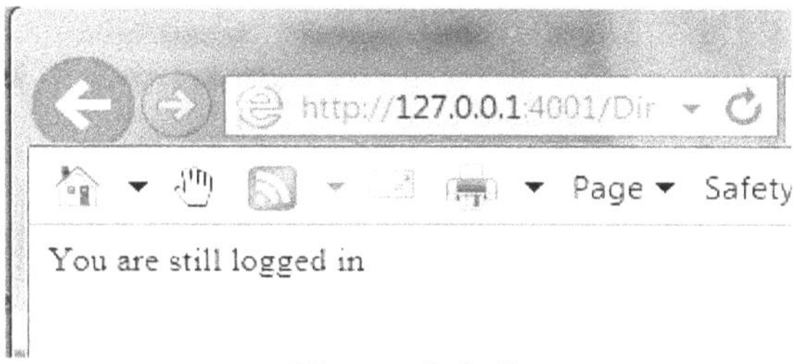

Figure 9.2.5

Lesson 9.3 - Overview of Sessions.

An alternative to using cookies to store data over a series of web pages is sessions. The difference with cookies is that while the cookie stores data on the client side, sessions store data on the server side.

Sessions have some advantages over cookies:
- Since the session data is stored on the server, it is more secure. The session is store on the server side so the data is not being transmitted or potentially available to others who have gained access to the client side computer.
- Sessions can store data for browsers that do not accept cookies.
- More information can be stored in a session than in a cookie.

When a session is created a random session ID is created and sent to the client as a cookie. The ID is a string of 32 hexidecimal characters and is stored in a cookie called PHPSESSID. Pages requiring this information can reference this ID to obtain the session data.

Sessions may also be created without cookies. The ID can be appended to the URL in each hyperlink to other pages on the website. This may be more reliable than cookies since many users have set their browsers to decline cookies.

Lesson 9.4 - Using Sessions.

When setting up a session the session_start() function must be executed. Once session has started data can be stored to or extracted from the session. In the first example a session is started and then the field view is set to 1.

```
1   <?php
2       session_start();        // must start session first
3       $_SESSION['view'] = 1;
4       echo('Views: ' . $_SESSION['view']);
5   ?>
```

Views: 1

Figure 9.4.1

In the example (Figure 9.4.1), note that the first instruction starts the session, the second instruction sets a variable named 'view' to a value of 1. This instruction declares the variable if it does not exist in the session, if it exists it will insert a value of 1 into that variable. The last instruction prints out the string literal "Views: " and the contents of the session found in the $_SESSION variable named 'view'.

Next, we will show an example on how to add a value to an existing SESSION variable if it exists or if it does not exist, it creates the variable and sets it.

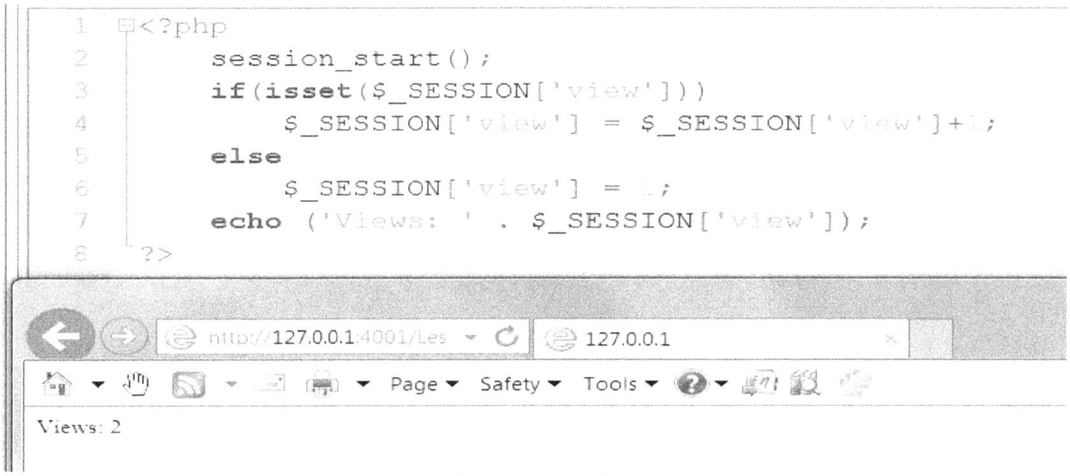

```
1   <?php
2       session_start();
3       if(isset($_SESSION['view']))
4           $_SESSION['view'] = $_SESSION['view']+1;
5       else
6           $_SESSION['view'] = 1;
7       echo ('Views: ' . $_SESSION['view']);
8   ?>
```

Views: 2

Figure 9.4.2

This example starts the session and then tests to see if the variable exists and has a value using the isset() function. If the variable exists with a value, 1 is added to the variable. If it does not exist, the variable is established and set to 1. The last instruction shows the current value of the affected variable.

In cases where a variable is no longer needed the programmer can issue the unset() function. This function removes the variable from the session ($_SESSION).

```php
<?php
    session_start();
    if(isset($_SESSION['view']))
        unset($_SESSION['view']);
?>
```

Figure 9.4.3

The code shows a test to see if a variable named 'view' exists in the session. If it exists, the unset() statement removes 'view' from $_SESSION. The run below is the same php program that was run in Figure 9.4.1, that declared the variable 'view' and set it to 1.

The next example shows only the code. I do not recommend using this without understanding and recognizing that this deletes the session it opens. Test this thoroughly before using.

```php
<?php
    session_start();
    session_destroy();
?>
```

Now lets create several variables in a session. After the variables have been created and initialized with some values, display the contents of the variables in the session.

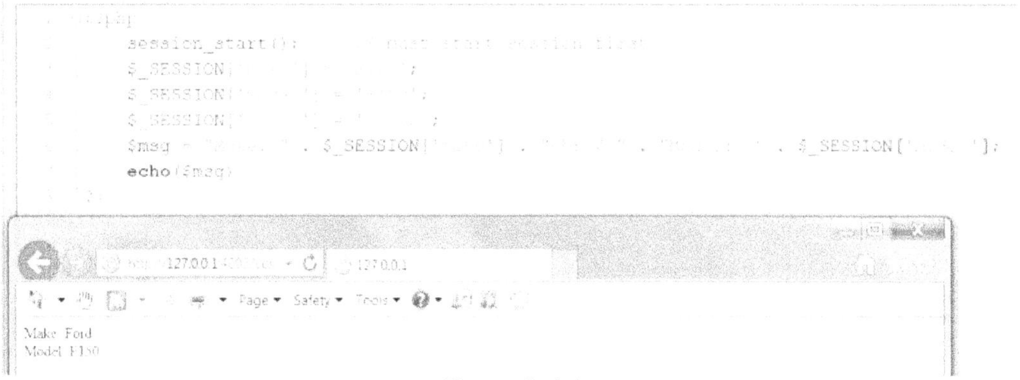

Figure 9.4.4

Session variables may also be arrays. Our example here declares an array named $cars and places the names of three car makers in that array. The variable 'make' is loaded with the array values, a variable 'type' and one named 'color' are named and given values. The last statement will display the values it finds.

83

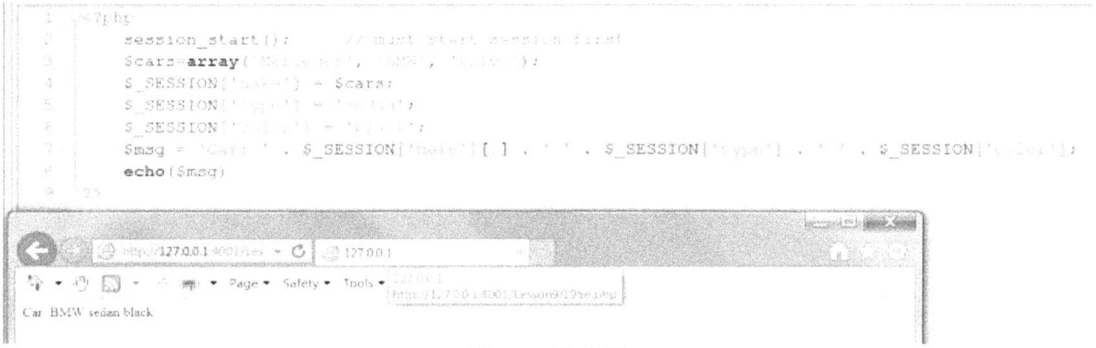

```
1   <?php
2       session_start();      // must start session first
3       $cars=array('Mercedes', 'BMW', 'Volvo');
4       $_SESSION['make'] = $cars;
5       $_SESSION['type'] = 'sedan';
6       $_SESSION['color'] = 'black';
7       $msg = 'Car: ' . $_SESSION['make'][ ] . ' ' . $_SESSION['type'] . ' ' . $_SESSION['color']);
8       echo($msg)
9   ?>
```

Car BMW sedan black

Figure 9.4.5

Note that the car maker it picked from the array is the second car in the array 'BMW'. To display a specific array element you need to specify which element. The statement in line 7 shows the selection of Cars: as $_SESSION['make'][1]. The [1] tells it to select the second element because arrays all begin with element [0] (they are zero based). This means if the program was to select 'Mercedes' the statement would read $_SESSION['make'][0].

How do you see all of the contents of all of the variables in a session?. The next example shows the contents of the session we have created in this lesson. The statement `Print-r($_SESSION)` shows all of the entries in the current session ($_SESSION).

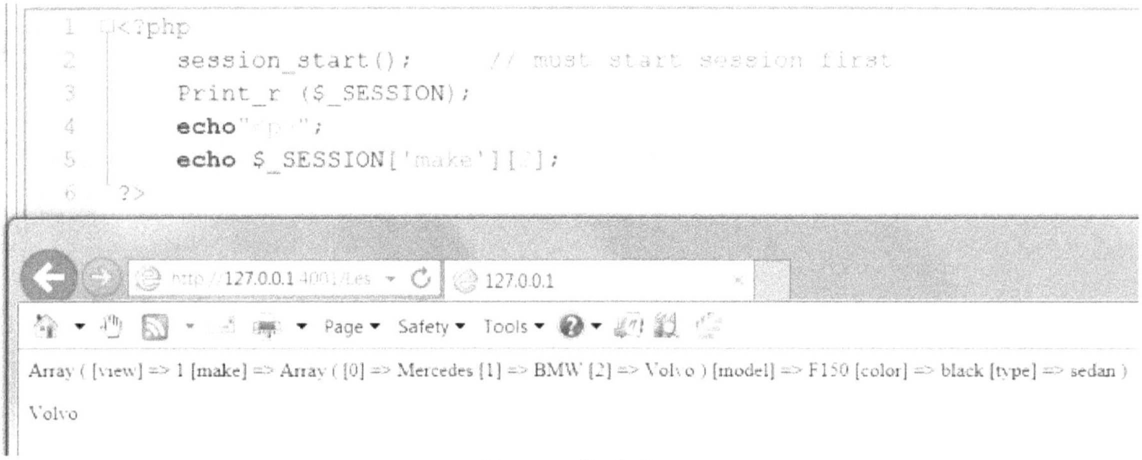

```
1   <?php
2       session_start();      // must start session first
3       Print_r ($_SESSION);
4       echo" ";
5       echo $_SESSION['make'][ ];
6   ?>
```

Array ([view] => 1 [make] => Array ([0] => Mercedes [1] => BMW [2] => Volvo) [model] => F150 [color] => black [type] => sedan)

Volvo

Figure 9.4.6

Examine the output carefully. The array established in $_SESSION shows the contents of the variable 'view'; the elements of our 'make' array (all 3 values with their element numbers); the variable 'model', the variable 'color' and the variable 'type' and the current contents of the variables.

Lesson 9.5 - Cookies or Sessions?

Now that we have created cookies and sessions, which shall we choose?. The answer can be simple or can be complex. Look at the advantages of each, don't discount either until you carefully consider both. The first thing to consider is the type of data to be transmitted. Is security an issue. Then how much data is required. If ease of creation and there is no security requirement, you could create several cookies to make up the storage limitations.

84

The browser that blocks cookies can be a determination of using cookies or sessions. However, it is common to request that the user accept cookies to use your web sites. Consider the alternatives and make a good decision based on the facts and application requirements.

Advantages of cookies:
       Easier to create
       Easier to read
       Less overhead on the server
       Usually persist over longer periods of time.

Advantages of sessions:
       More secure.
       Less data transmitted.
       Larger storage capacity.
       Can work even if browser blocks cookies.

Study the advantages, try creating both cookies and sessions, make an informed decision.

Lesson 9.6 - Random Numbers.

Random numbers are generated by the rand() function. The rand() function can generate a random number between 0 and the maximum number allowed by the version of php you are using as determined in the php parameter which can be displayed by the getrandmax() function. The rand() function may also limit the numbers produced by including a min and max parameter, rand(min, max). The example below will generate 3 random numbers between 0 and the php maximum number then generate a random number between 1 and 6 and lastly generate a random number between 1 and 100.

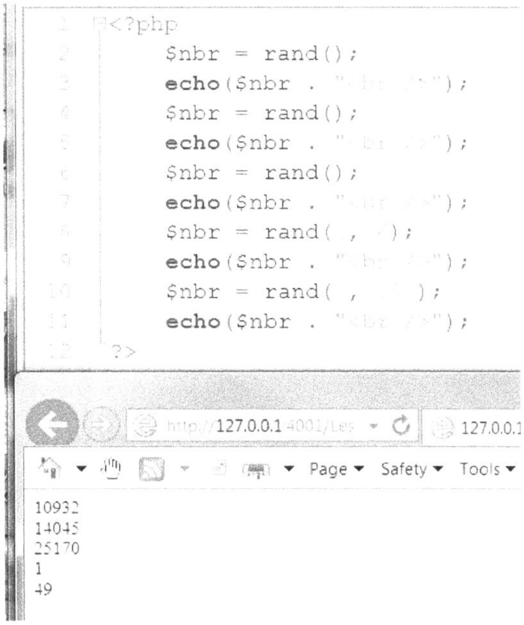

Figure 9.6.1

85

Random numbers may also be generated by the mt_rand() function. In Figure 9.6.2 we see a comparison of rand() and mt_rand().

```
1  <?php
2      $nbr = rand();
3      echo($nbr . "<br />");
4      $nbr = mt_rand();
5      echo("Now mt-rand(): ");
6      echo($nbr . "<br />");
7  ?>
```

http://127.0.0.1:4001/Les ▼ ○   127.0.0.

🏠 ▼ 🖨 📰 ▼ 🖳 🖶 ▼ Page ▼ Safety ▼ Tools ▼

13899
Now mt-rand(): 683844802

Figure 9.6.2

The advantage of the mt-rand() random number generator is a better random number and the generation is 4 times faster. The speed and accuracy is important especially important in gaming applications.

The rand() function can be used for games, random quotes, and many other situations involve random numbers. PHP provides the rand() function to make it easy to create random numbers. The syntax for this function is:

rand(lowerbound, upperbound);

The two arguments lowerbound and upperbound signify the range of numbers to be created. Lowerbound is the lowest number in the range and upperbound is the highest number in the range created by the rand() function.

The following program simulates rolling two dice, totaling the numbers generated (1 to 6), printing the number generated for each die, the total of the two numbers, and if it is Wednesday, print out the message "See You Thursday!". If it is any other day other than Wednesday the program prints out the message "Have a nice day!".

```
<html>
<head>
    <title>Dice Program </title>
</head>
<body>
<h1>Dice Program</h1>
<p>
    <?php
    $die1 = rand(1, 6);
    $die2 = rand(1, 6);
    // Got 2 random numbers between 1 and 6;
    $total = $die1 + $die2;
```

86

```php
        echo "Die Number One " . $die1;
        echo "<br />";
        echo "Die Number Two " . $die2;
        echo "<br />";
        echo "The total of the two dice is: " . $total;
        echo "<br />";
        ?>
        </p>
        <?php
        $d=date("D");
        if ($d=="Wed")
                echo "See You Thursday!";
        else
                echo "Have a nice day!";
        ?>
</p>
</body>
</html>
```

Next we look at two runs of the above program. Run the program and then click on the refresh icon for additional runs of the program without reloading.

Run #1

Figure 9.6.1

Run #2

Figure 9.6.2

The PHP rand function that generates the numbers are:

87

```
$die1 = rand(1, 6);
$die2 = rand(1, 6);
```

The lowerbound for both is 1 and the upperbound for both is 6. Once the numbers are generated and stored in a variable, they can be used for arithmetic, printing or in any other legal PHP statement or function parameter.

Lesson 9.7 - Summary.

Cookies or Sessions, which do we choose? Look at the advantages of each, security, capacity, ease of use, you need to make the decision. In today's world, perhaps security trumps. Even if security may not be your main issue, it may be important to the user and usually that determines what happens.

Random numbers are important in gaming and other applications that may be found online, like showing random pictures or text.

In Review:

1. A cookie is a _____ that can be stored on the client computer.
   a.   database
   b.   picture
   c.   text file
   d.   some sweet code
2. Only the program that placed the cookie on the client can use the contents of the cookie.
   a.   True
   b.   False
3. PHP creates cookies with the _____ function.
   a.   createcookie()
   b.   setcookie()
   c.   cookie()
   d.   newcookie()
4. The function that sets the cookie must be placed:
   a.   in its own PHP program
   b.   at the end of all code
   c.   before any other code
   d.   in a function by itself
5. _____ store data on the server side
   a.   cookies
   b.   sessions
   c.   HTML
   d.   none of the above
6. _____ can store data for browsers that do not accept _____.
   a.   plugins, cookies
   b.   plugins, sessions
   c.   sessions, plugins
   d.   sessions, cookies
7. A session creates an ID as a string of _____ characters.
   a.   8
   b.   16
   c.   32
   d.   64
8. Which is not an advantage of cookies?
   a.   easy to create
   b.   easy to read
   c.   less data transmitted
   d.   usually persist over longer periods of time
9. Which is not an advantage of sessions?
   a.   more secure
   b.   less overhead on the server
   c.   larger storage capacity
   d.   can work even if browser blocks cookies
10. Random numbers are created by the _____ function.
   a.   rand()
   b.   random()
   c.   srand()
   d.   randnum()

Start Programming with PHP

An Introduction to PHP and MySQL

LESSON 10: Coding PHP

Lesson 10.1 - Overview

Up to this point we have only played with enough code to illustrate the current lessons concepts. Now we will look at larger PHP programs. Actually we will look at groups of related programs and learn how we can create reusable code. Write and test the code and when it is working, use the working code wherever it is needed.

Lesson 10.2 – External Files.

Breaking up PHP programs by creating separate pages for particular elements common to several pages or parts of pages will save development time. There are always some common elements that can be broken out into separate files and then incorporated into each web page that requires those elements. Some more obvious elements may be headers, footers, file management, navigation, etc.. All elements that are common to several different pages should be considered for external files.

These elements may then be incorporated into web pages using one of two functions:

```
        include()
                or
        require()
```

The include() function generates a warning if it fails, but the script continues to run. If the require() function fails the script terminates.

Lesson 10.3 – Parts of Code

Including Headings, footers, and parts of code is a popular use of the include() and require() statements. For example, every page of a web site may have exactly the same information. This is an ideal application for an include() function. Navigation bars another candidate, since they should all be alike to conform to good practices. Almost any code that is used more than once in a web site could be a candidate for the include() or require() functions.

Another possible use is for text that changes frequently. The text is put into a text file and the file is then included in the web site. Each time the text changes, a new text file is swapped in and the web site has been updated.

Another common use is to code frequently used php scripts and include them whenever needed. One example is a php script that puts the date and time on a web page. Write and test it once and used it any time it is needed.

Lesson 10.4 – Example Routines

The example program is a HTML program shown in Figure 10.4.1. We will segregate the program into 3 parts. The header, the footer, and the changeable code. That means we will generate 3 scripts for the index page and then use the header and footer for the Products page, the Login page and the Register page. This builds consistency of header and footer information for all four pages.

First the complete HTML page that we will use to break out the header and footer.

```
<!DOCTYPE html PUBLIC "-//W3C//DTD XHTML 1.0 Transitional//EN"
"http://www.w3.org/TR/xhtml1/DTD/
xhtml1-transitional.dtd">

<html xmlns="http://www.w3.org/1999/xhtml" xml:lang="en" lang="en">
<head>
<meta http-equiv="content-type"
content="text/html; charset=utf-8" />
<title>PHP Programming Association</title>
<style type="text/css">
      body {
            margin: 0px 0px 0px 0px;
            background: #9f9;
            }
      #leftcontent {
            float:left;
            width:67%;
            background:#fff;
            border-right:2px solid #000;
            border-bottom: 2px solid #000;
            margin-right:15px;
            padding-bottom:20px;
            }
      p,h1,pre {
            margin:0px 30px 10px 30px;
            }
      h1 {
            font-size:14px;
            padding-top:10px;
            }
      #rightcontent p {
            font-size:14px;
            margin-left:0px;
            }
</style>
</head>
<body>
<div id="leftcontent">

<!-- BEGIN CHANGEABLE CONTENT -->
<h1>PHP Programming Association</h1>
<p>Lorem ipsum dolor sit amet, consectetur adipiscing elit. Aenean ut fermentum
augue, at vehicula lectus. Nunc quis ligula bibendum, commodo odio eu, pretium sem.
Vivamus venenatis ligula est, in condimentum justo ultrices non. Mauris eleifend
dui vel lorem ultrices dictum. Quisque turpis mauris, viverra non consequat vitae,
blandit in libero.
</p>
<p>Vivamus vitae tellus elementum, feugiat erat sed, rutrum dolor. In metus nisl,
```

91

```
consequat at laoreet quis, scelerisque et erat. Pellentesque habitant morbi
tristique senectus et netus et malesuada fames ac turpis egestas. Nam eleifend dui
leo, et faucibus tellus placerat vel.
</p>
<p>Donec tempus ullamcorper massa, pulvinar bibendum arcu viverra eu. Proin et arcu
nibh. Nam pellentesque porta vestibulum.
</p>
<!-- END OF CHANGEABLE CONTENT →

</div>
<div id="rightcontent">
<h1>Navigation</h1>
<p><a href="index.php">Home</a><br />
<a href="tutorials.php">Products</a><br />
<a href="login.php">Login</a><br />
<a href="register.php">Register</a></p>
</div>
</body>
</html>
```

When it is run we see Figure 10.4.1.

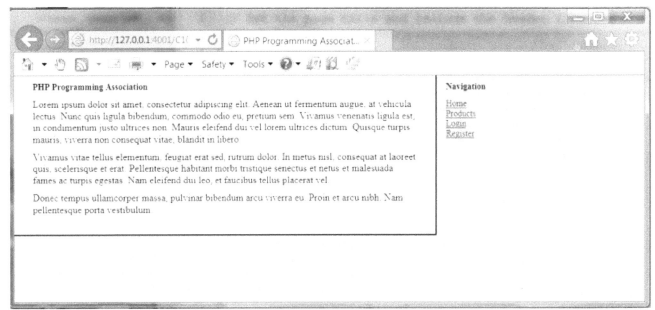

Figure 10.4.1

Looking at the code there are two comments in the code that bracket the "CHANGEABLE CODE".
This is the area of the basic web site template that will change when using the templates. The
first part of the code above this area we will put in a file called "header.php" and the second part
that is after the changeable code we will put in a file called "footer.php".

The header code is here:

```
<!DOCTYPE html PUBLIC "-//W3C//DTD XHTML 1.0 Transitional//EN"
"http://www.w3.org/TR/xhtml1/DTD/
xhtml1-transitional.dtd">

<html xmlns="http://www.w3.org/1999/xhtml" xml:lang="en" lang="en">
```

```
<head>
<meta http-equiv="content-type"
content="text/html; charset=utf-8" />
<title>PHP Programming Association</title>
<style type="text/css">
        body {
                margin: 0px 0px 0px 0px;
                background: #9f9;
                }
        #leftcontent {
                float:left;
                width:67%;
                background:#fff;
                border-right:2px solid #000;
                border-bottom: 2px solid #000;
                margin-right:15px;
                padding-bottom:20px;
                }
        p,h1,pre {
                margin:0px 30px 10px 30px;
                }
        h1 {
                font-size:14px;
                padding-top:10px;
                }
        #rightcontent p {
                font-size:14px;
                margin-left:0px;
                }
</style>
</head>
<body>
<div id="leftcontent">
<!--Script - header.html -->
<!-- BEGIN CHANGEABLE CONTENT -->
```

The code for footer.php is here:

```
<!-- END OF CHANGEABLE CONTENT -->
<!-- Script footer.html -->
</div>

<div id="rightcontent">
<h1>Navigation</h1>
<p><a href="index.php">Home</a><br />
<a href="tutorials.php">Products</a><br />
<a href="login.php">Login</a><br />
<a href="register.php">Register</a></p>
</div>
</body>
</html>
```

Now the code for the index file looks like this:

```
<?php // Script - Xindex.php
/* This is the home page for this site
```

```
It uses templates to create the layout */

//include the header
require('templates/header.html');
//leave the PHP section to display lots of HTML
?>


<h1>PHP Programming Association</h1>
<p>Lorem ipsum dolor sit amet, consectetur adipiscing elit. Aenean ut fermentum
augue, at vehicula lectus. Nunc quis ligula bibendum, commodo odio eu, pretium sem.
Vivamus venenatis ligula est, in condimentum justo ultrices non. Mauris eleifend
dui vel lorem ultrices dictum. Quisque turpis mauris, viverra non consequat vitae,
blandit in libero.
</p>
<p>Vivamus vitae tellus elementum, feugiat erat sed, rutrum dolor. In metus nisl,
consequat at laoreet quis, scelerisque et erat. Pellentesque habitant morbi
tristique senectus et netus et malesuada fames ac turpis egestas. Nam eleifend dui
leo, et faucibus tellus placerat vel.
</p>
<p>Donec tempus ullamcorper massa, pulvinar bibendum arcu viverra eu. Proin et arcu
nibh. Nam pellentesque porta vestibulum.
</p>


<?php //Return to PHP
require('templates/footer.html'); // include the footer
?>
```

The program uses require() function to include the header and footer information.

To set up this demo we need to properly construct the structure so the code will work. In the directory containing the script Xindex.php, create a new directory named "templates". Put the scripts named header.html and footer.html in the new "templates" folder. Now, you are ready to run.

When we run the application we see:

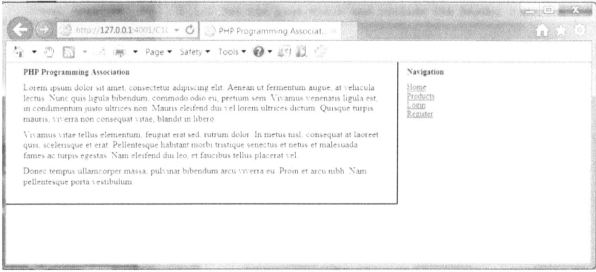

Figure 10.4.2

94

Amazing! It looks just like the original.

Now we will take a peek at the other 3 pages of this web site. Products, Login, and Register. We will look at the code and then the result when it runs.

Products Code:

```php
<?php // Script - tutorials.php
/*This page lists our Tutorials. */

// Set the page title and include the header file
define('TITLE', 'PHP Programming Association');
require('templates/header.html');

// Leave the PHP section to display lots of HTML
?>
<h1>Tutorials</h1>
<p><ul>
     <li>Alice Programming</li>
     <li>Visual Basic.NET</li>
     <li>C++</li>
     <li>Python</li>
     <li>PHP</li>
     <li>HTML5/CSS3</li>
     <li>Java</li>
</ul></p>

<?php // Return to PHP and include the footer
require('templates/footer.html');
?>
```

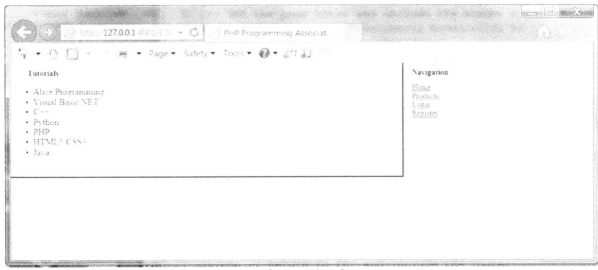

Figure 10.4.3

Now create a more complicated version of header and footer. We will name these new files header2 and footer2 and place them in the "templates" folder.

header2.php Code

```
<!DOCTYPE html PUBLIC "-//W3C//DTD XHTML 1.0 Transitional//EN"
"http://www.w3.org/TR/xhtml1/DTD/
xhtml1-transitional.dtd">

<html xmlns="http://www.w3.org/1999/xhtml" xml:lang="en" lang="en">
<head>
<meta http-equiv="content-type"
content="text/html; charset=utf-8" />
<title>
<?php
        if (defined('TITLE')) {
                print TITLE;
        } else {
                print 'PHP Programming Association';
        }
?>
</title>
<style type="text/css">
        body {
                margin: 0px 0px 0px 0px;
                background: #c9c9fc;
                }
        #leftcontent {
                float:left;
                width:67%;
                background:#fff;
                border-right:2px solid #000;
                border-bottom: 2px solid #000;
                margin-right:15px;
                padding-bottom:20px;
                }
        p,h1,pre {
                margin:0px 30px 10px 30px;
                }
        h1 {
                font-size:14px;
                padding-top:10px;
                }
        #rightcontent p {
                font-size:14px;
                margin-left:0px;
                }
</style>
</head>
<body>
<div id="leftcontent">
<!--Script 8.2 - header.html -->
<!-- BEGIN CHANGEABLE CONTENT -->
```

footer2.php Code

Login Code:

```php
<?php // Script 8.8 - login.php
define('TITLE', 'login');
require('templates/header2.html');

print '<h1>Login Form</h1>
      <p>Users who are logged in can take advantage of certain features like this,
that, and
      the other thing.</p>';

if ( isset($_POST['submitted'])) {
// Handle the form
if (( !empty($_POST['email'])) && (!empty($_POST['password']))) {
      if ((strtolower($_POST['email']) == 'me@example.com') && ($_POST['password']
==
      'textpass')) { // correct
            print '<p>You are logged in!<br />Now you can blah, blah, blah...
</p>';
      } else {
            print '<p>The submitted email address and password do not match those
on file!<br />
            Go back and try again. </p>';
      }
} else {   // Incorrect
      print '<p>Please make sure you enter both an email address and a password!<br
/>
      Go back and try again.</p>';
      }
} else {   // Forgot a field
      print '<form action="Login.php" method="POST">
      <p>Email Address: <input type="text" name="email" size="20" /></p>
      <p>Password: <input type="password" name="password" size="20" /></p>
      <p><input type="submit" name="submit" value="Log In" /></p>
      <input type="hidden" name="submitted" value="true" />
      </form>';

}

require('templates/footer2.html'); // need the footer
?>
```

97

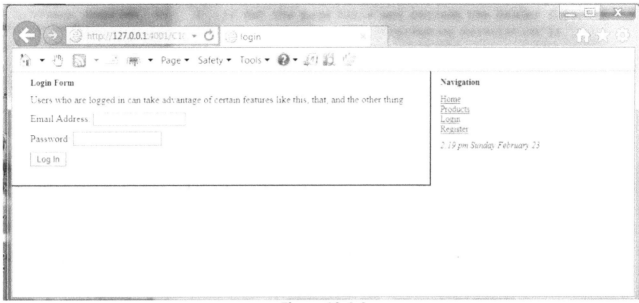

Figure 10.4.4

Register Code:

```php
<?php // Script 8.9 - register.php
define('Title', 'Register');
require('templates/header2.html');

// Print introductory text
print '<h1>Registration Form</h1>
    <p>Register so that you can take advantage of our
    famous tutorials.</p>';

// Add the CSS
print '<style type="text/css" media="Screen">
    .error {color:red; }
</style>';

if ( isset($_POST['submitted'])) {
    $problem = FALSE;

    if (empty($_POST['first_name'])) {
        $problem = TRUE;
        print '<p class="error">Please Enter
        your first name</p>';
    }

    if (empty($_POST['last_name'])) {
        $problem = TRUE;
        print '<p class="error">Please Enter
        your last name</p>';
    }

    if (empty($_POST['email'])) {
        $problem = TRUE;
        print '<p class="error">Please Enter
        your email address</p>';
```

```php
    }

    if (empty($_POST['password1'])) {
        $problem = TRUE;
        print '<p class="error">Please Enter
        your password</p>';
    }

    if ($_POST['password1'] != $_POST['password2']) {
        $problem = TRUE;
        print '<p class="error">Passwords do not match</p>';
    }

    if (!$problem)  { // If there were no problems
        // print a message
        print '<p>You are now registered <br />Okay, you are not really
registered but it was good practice.</p>';

        // clear the posted values
        $_POST == array();
    } else {  // Forget a field
        print '<p class="error">Please try again.</p>';
    }

    } // End of form handle form if

    // Create the form
    ?>
    <form action="register.php" method="POST">

    <p>First Name: <input type="text" name="first_name" size="20" value="<?php if
(isset($_POST['first_name']))
    { print htmlspecialchars($_POST['first_name']); } ?>" /></p>

    <p>Last Name: <input type="text" name="last_name" size="20" value="<?php if
(isset($_POST
    ['last_name'])) { print htmlspecialchars($_POST['last_name']); } ?>" /></p>

    <p>Email Address: <input type="text" name="email" size="20" value="<?php if
(isset($_POST
    ['email'])) { print htmlspecialchars($_POST['email']); } ?>" /></p>

    <p>Password: <input type="password" name="password1" size="20" /></p>
    <p>Confirm Password: <input type="password" name="password2" size="20" /></p>
    <input type="submit" name="submit" value="Register" /></p>
    <input type="hidden" name="submitted" value="true" />
    </form>
<?php require('templates/footer2.html'); // Need the footer  ?>
```

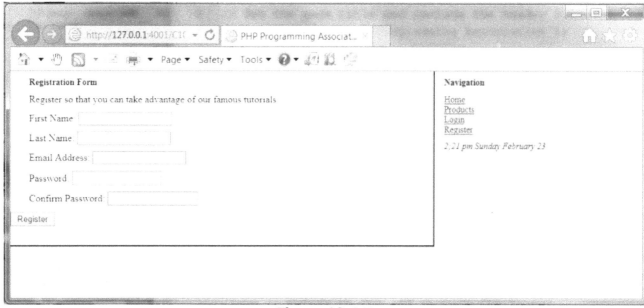

Figure 10.4.5

For those who are more observant, there are two versions of the header and footer in use here. The second version of the footer added the date and time to the bottom of the Navigation links. The second version of the header did a little more error checking. The header.php and footer.php will work just as well for our purposes.

Lesson 10.5 - Summary.

Using PHP with HTML provides for dynamic web sites and for inclusion of php routines to allow the use of generalized code where it applies to several or even all web pages on a web site. The include() function allows the code to continue if the included code is not available. The required() function insures the code is found or it will not render the web page.

In Review:

1. All elements that are common to several different pages can be incorporated from an external file into those pages by using:
    a.   include()
    b.   require()
    c.   both a and b
    d.   none of the above

2. The _____ function generates a warning if it fails, but the script continues to run.
    a.   include()
    b.   require()
    c.   both a and b
    d.   none of the above

3. If the _____ function fails, the script terminates.
    a.   include()
    b.   require()
    c.   both a and b
    d.   none of the above

Start Programming with PHP

An Introduction to PHP and MySQL

Lesson 11 – MySQL - Administering the Database

Lesson 11.1 - An Introduction to MySQL:

MySQL is one of the most popular databases used for web based databases. It is a robust database management system that can handle significant transaction loads as found in Internet applications and best of all you can obtain MySQL for FREE!. MySQL is one of the freebies that is a premier software with a lot of documentation and it adheres to the SQL syntax. MySQL is often paired with the PHP programming language and they form a formidable Internet tool.

A common acronym in Internet parlance is LAMP. This stands for four significant yet free Internet products used to comprise a web server. L is for Linux; A is for Apache web server; M is for MySQL; and P is for the programming language PHP. There are other variants XAMPP substitutes X for the OS because it is designed for several operating systems (Windows, Mac OS X, BSD and UNIX variants) and the last P is for the PERL programming language, also a free product. The LAMP structure is a major portion of the web servers running on today's Internet. Google the LAMP acronym and see the amount of documentation available on the web.

MySQL was developed by Michael Wedenius, Allan Larsson and David Axmark as an Open Source project. They have also built a business MySQL AB to develop MySQL and related products. MySQL is available as an Open Source, free product and there is also a commercial product (for companies who wish to deploy MySQL commercially in a closed source application).

The database includes an interactive, command-line client to interact with the server. MySQL supports the open standard ANSI SQL 99. There are also a number of GUI clients available both commercially and Open Source, available for those who do not feel comfortable working from the command line.

I have recommended using the WampServer product on a desktop as it contains everything you will need to run the examples, do the labs and go forth and be a successful MySQL developer. However, being more practical, one of the products that run on a USB drive may be a better choice. Look at XAMPP, Server2Go, and WOS. The same functions but your development environment follows you around. Perhaps the one thing that people struggle with in relating these exercises from doing it on one PC to doing MySQL on the Internet is the perspective. In our examples the single computer is acting as both the client and the server. Your web browser will be talking to the internal Apache server who in turn communicates with the MySQL engine. So, your computer is functioning in a dual role.

If you have a web hosting service, find out if they support MySQL. If the don't you should probably consider switching to one who does. I use: http://www.siteground.com and http://www.1and1.com for my web sites. Using one of these sites will help you really understand how a web based database works.

Web based databases are probably one of the most important concepts in database technology today. Many corporations are moving to web based databases to allow them to use the Internet to share their databases world wide. We also use web based databases when we shop one the web, when we use a course management system such as Moodle or Sakai or Blackboard, when we go to YouTube or pick out our favorite online music. There are also many content management systems used for web development like WordPress, Joomla and Drupal that will interact with online databases. As you can see it is vitally important to understand this direction in database technology to obtain employment in the industry.

The lessons on MySQL require using the command line. While tools like PHPMySQL and others, make database creation and maintenance easy, I feel it is important to understand MySQL from the command line as that is what happens in a PHP program. So, make sure you understand MySQL from the command line before venturing into writing PHP programs to create and maintain MySQL databases.

Lesson 11.2 - Database Administration

Systems Administration of a database is an important job. Add new users, make sure they can get to the data they need to do their job, yet prohibit them from accessing data they don't need to see. This is the responsibility of the database administrator. Not everyone who accesses the database should have administrative privileges. Remember when using a database in a web scenario, a program accesses the database for the user and access to functions in the database for software must be carefully considered.

Creating New Users

Once we have created a database we need to allow users to access the database. So, we need to create some users. Users should all have passwords and be given privileges according to their needs in using the database.

When you create a username you should follow some basic rules. First, there should be NO spaces in the username however you may substitute the underscore (_) character. Next there is a maximum of 16 characters. Lastly names are case sensitive.

Usernames should be descriptive, easy to remember and if you have many users, it is important to standardize how you compose names. For example, use the user's first initial and last name or their first and last initial and their employee number. If one of these are used it should apply to all users in the company.

After installing MySQL you should establish a password for the root account. The root account can do anything that can be done with a database including dropping tables and databases from MySQL. This is a potential danger and this type of access should be limited. I recommend that the root user only be used in the most dire circumstances. Set up an administrator account that can create, delete, drop, tables and databases to protect root and its password. The command to establish a root password is:

```
mysql> SET PASSWORD FOR 'root'@'localhost' = PASSWORD('password');
```

This will create the password you supply to the root account and you will need that when you try to access MySQL as the root user.

The password has no length restrictions but is case-sensitive. They are encrypted by the MySQL database when they are stored. It is possible to create a user with no password but this practice should be avoided.

Privileges

Privileges are used to increase the security of the database. They insure the proper level of authority for each user. If a user does not need to do something they are not granted that privilege. A person designated to input data into the system may only have the privileges to SELECT, INSERT and UPDATE assigned to them. A person who administers the database may have more extensive privileges or perhaps be granted all privileges.

A PHP program that accesses the MySQL database may be granted only SELECT privileges as that is all that is needed to create a report or select data for a web site. Granting privileges to programs, especially programs that service web requests should be carefully considered. Programs may have several different users available for processing depending if they are in a mode when they are selecting data or updating data. If a program is to updata data that user should open, update the data and then be immediately closed.

MySQL Privileges

Privilege	Allows
SELECT	Reads rows from tables
INSERT	Adds new rows of data to databases
UPDATE	Alter existing data in tables
DELETE	Remove existing data from tables
INDEX	Create and drop indexes to tables
ALTER	Modify the structure of a table
CREATE	Create new tables or databases
DROP	Delete existing tables or databases
RELOAD	Reload the grant tables (and therefore enact user changes).
SHUTDOWN	Stop the MySQL server
PROCESS	View and stop existing MySQL processes.
FILE	Import data into tables from text files
GRANT	Create new users
REVOKE	Remove users' permissions
ALL	User has all privileges.

The bottom line is to make sure the user has ONLY those privileges that they need to do the job. The same goes for programs. Users or programs with privileges over and above what they need can lead to a security breach.

There are a number of different ways to create users and grant them privileges. Perhaps one of the most used way is through phpMyAdmin GUI interface.

However, in this lesson we will look at ways to create users and grant privileges from the command line or from a PHP program. There are a few different ways and we need to explore the most used.

Basic Syntax for creating a user:

```
CREATE USER 'username'@'localhost' IDENTIFIED BY 'password';
```

The rules for the username are:

No spaces in the username, only letters, numbers and the underscore (_) character.
A maximum of 16 characters.
Names are case sensitive

The syntax @'localhost' indicates that this user can only access the database from the localhost MySQL server. If the database is running on another server, substitute the name of that server.

The password rules are as follows:

No specific length constraints
Passwords are case sensitive
Contains letters, numbers and special characters.
If you omit the IDENTIFIED BY clause, a password will not be required. (AVOID)
Eight characters or more composed of letters, numbers and special characters is best.

EXAMPLE:

```
mysql> CREATE USER 'jack'@'localhost' IDENTIFIED BY 'quick123';
Query OK, 0 rows affected (0.00 sec)
mysql>
```

Then to grant privileges of SELECT, INSERT and UPDATE on a database named work, to this user you could use:

```
mysql> GRANT SELECT, INSERT, UPDATE on work.* TO 'jack';
```

Another way to create a user and grant all privileges in one command is also available.

EXAMPLE:

```
mysql> GRANT ALL PRIVILEGES
    -> on work.*
    -> To 'jill'@'localhost'
    -> IDENTIFIED BY 'hill543';
```

This command sequence grants all privileges to the database named work to a user named jill with a password of hill543.

Another way with more explicit grants may look like this:

EXAMPLE:

```
mysql>GRANT SELECT, INSERT, UPDATE,
    ->DELETE, CREATE, DROP, ALTER, INDEX
    ->ON work.* TO 'bill'@'localhost'
    ->IDENTIFIED BY 'boards444';
Query OK, 0 rows affected (0.00 sec)
```

There are many different ways to create users and grant privileges and you can use any one to achieve your results. However, the thing to remember is that the privileges are the security issue and should be considered carefully and granted prudently.

Lesson 11.3 - Create A Database

Before we can do anything we must have planned out our database, tables, normalization, etc.. For the purposes of our course we have already done this and are now prepared to start building our "School" database. This will contain, student, course, grade information for our internet school.

```
First we create the database container to hold all of our tables.  This is done
with the CREATE DATABASE command.  In MySQL it will look something like this:

     mysql> create database school;
```

NOTE: MySQL requires all command lines to end in a semi-colon (;). If you forget this, the command will not work.

After you type in the command and hit enter the screen should look something like this:

```
     mysql> create database school;
     Query OK, 1 row affected (0.02 sec)
```

If you did not get the proper response, make sure you entered a semicolon after school and before you hit enter. Repeat the command until you successfully create the database. To check this use the command SHOW DATABASES;.

```
     mysql>show databases;
     +-----------------------------------+
     | Database                          |
     +-----------------------------------+
     | mysql                             |
     | school                            |
     +-----------------------------------+
     2 rows in set (0.00 sec)
```

This should confirm the existence of your database. It will be required to do subsequent steps. Note, the MySQL database is required by MySQL for tracking important components. There may also be a database named test. Please do not delete any of these databases.

Lesson 11.4 - SQL Data Types & Field Modifiers

To understand how to build a table we need to review some of the basics of different data types and modifiers present in most programming languages. MySQL has a list of data types with the range of data allowed in each data type as well as for additional customization of the field. Some of the allowable data types are in the following table:

Type	Description
int	Whole Numbers from -2147483648 to 2147483647
decimal	Floating point numbers – decimal(4, 2) allows values -99.99 to 99.99
double	Double-precision floating point number
date	A date in YYYY-MM-DD format
time	A time in HH:MM:SS format
datetime	A date and time in the format: YYYY-MM-DD HH:MM:SS

Type	Description
text	A string up to 65535 characters in length.
char	A fixed length string of up to 255 characters char(12) will always allow for a 12 character string.
varchar	A defined string of variable length up to 255 characters. The field will only contain the actual number of characters entered.
blob	Binary data type
Enum	A single string value in a defined list enum("cat", "dog", "fish", "horse) allows only the entry of those four types of animals. You could not enter "cow".

There are several other data types that will not be required for this course. Refer to MySQL documentation for more information on data types.

In addition to specifying allowable data types for each field there are several modifiers that can be used to further customize the field.

Modifier	Description
not null	Requires each record includes data entered in the column.
unique	Requires that data may not be duplicated in this column of the table.
auto_increment	Only for numeric data types, generates a unique number for each row.
primary key()	Requires the name of the column to be used as the primary key for that table. EXAMPLE: primary key(studentid) makes that field the unique primary key for that table.

Quite often more than one modifier may be used for a single field.

Lesson 11.5 - Create Database Tables

We have created a container for our data. Now we can normalize our data and create the normalized tables. We created a database named school and we will proceed to create some tables to store our data. Before we can create a table we must tell MySQL which database we want to address. Remember, MySQL can have many databases stored so you must be specific as to which database you want to use. You do this with the "use" command:

```
mysql>use school;
Database changed
```

MySQL has now informed us that it will direct all commands to the database named "school". Once we have been directed to the proper database we can proceed to create the various necessary tables.

Now we are ready to create our first table. The command for creating a table is as follows:

```
create table tablename (
```

```
fieldname1 data type modifiers,
fieldname2 data type modifiers,
*
*
fieldnamen data type modifiers);
```

Now lets apply this to a table we will call "students" that will contain the essential student data with a unique field named studentid that is the primary key.

```
create table students (
    studentid int unique primary key,
    studentlastname varchar(50),
    studentfirstname varchar(50),
    studentmajor char(3),
    studententry date);
```

After we execute this command we should get a message that looks like:

```
Query OK, 0 rows affected (0.00 sec)
```

When you want to see how a table is defined after it has been created you can use the "desc" command to show the fields in a table. The syntax for this command is:

```
desc tablename;
```

TO see the table we just created we need to issue the following command:

```
mysql>desc students;

+------------------+-------------+-------------------+------+------+---------+-----------+
| Field            | Type        | Collation         | Null | Key  | Default | Extra     |
+------------------+-------------+-------------------+------+------+---------+-----------+
|studentid         | int         | binary            | YES  | PRI  | NULL    |           |
|studentlastname   | varchar(50) | binary            | YES  |      | NULL    |           |
|studentfirstname  | varchar(50) | binary            | YES  |      | NULL    |           |
|studentmajor      | char(3)     | binary            | YES  |      | NULL    |           |
|studententry      | date        | binary            | YES  |      | NULL    |           |
+------------------+-------------+-------------------+------+------+---------+-----------+
5 rows in set (0.00 sec)
```

Your screen may not look exactly like this but it should be close.

With the creation of this table we can now insert students data into the table.

Lesson 11.6 - Summary

This lesson has outlined some of the administrative steps in starting your database. We did not go into detail on analysis and planning of the database. We did not go over normalization of the database. This omission was not to minimize the importance of those tasks. If you don't understand these steps you should review them before continuing. If you feel you are up to speed on these issues read on.

Whether the user is John in accounting or a php program, creating users and granting privileges is an important administrator task. Creating users and granting privileges can be done from the command line or from a GUI application like phpMyAdmin. Learning to use both is important to developers and administrators alike.

The root password must be protected at all cost. Compromising this password give a potential

108

intruder full access to all aspects of your database. The root password should be generated and then filed away, not to be used except in an extreme emergency. An administrator account should be set up and used for all administrative tasks. Again, another password to protect. The administrator should ideally have two accounts, one for creating databases, deleting databases and tables, doing shutdowns, granting privileges, viewing and stopping processes and any other administrative tasks. The second account for normal day to day work on the database.

In Review:

1. The acronym LAMP stands for:
      a.   Linux And MySQL, PHP
      b.   Linux Apache MySQL PHP
      c.   Linux And MySQL Perl
      d.   Learn Apache MySQL PHP
2. Users should all have passwords and be given _____ according to their needs in using the database
      a.   usernames
      b.   keys
      c.   privileges
      d.   access
3. _____ are used to increase the security of the database.
      a.   usernames
      b.   keys
      c.   tables
      d.   privileges
4. Creating users is simplified by using the _____ GUI interface.
      a.   Windows
      b.   OS/X
      c.   phpMyAdmin
      d.   phpMyInfo
5. Privileges are assigned using the _____ command.
      a.   create
      b.   grant
      c.   user
      d.   select
6. MySQL may contain several databases. The _____ command specifies which database you wish to access.
      a.   use
      b.   create
      c.   user
      d.   show
7. MySQL stores the data in _____.
      a.   containers
      b.   commands
      c.   tables
      d.   views
8. Databases and Tables are created using the _____ command.
      a.   select
      b.   create
      c.   use
      d.   show

9. The data type used to store floating-point numbers is _____.
    a.   integer
    b.   double
    c.   floating
    d.   variable
10. The data type used to store whole numbers is _____.
    a.   integer
    b.   double
    c.   float
    d.   variable

Start Programming with PHP

An Introduction to PHP and MySQL

Lesson 12 – Working with Data

Lesson 12.1 - Insert Data into a Table

To put data into a table we need to use another SQL command. The command is called the "insert" command. This may not be the easiest way to get data into a table from the command line, but this is usually the job of some GUI type interface or from a application program. The syntax for this statement is as follows:

```
insert into tablename (fieldlist) values (valueslist);
```

The fieldlist is a list of fields that correspond to the values shown in the valuelist. This can be entered from the command line or built by an application program. Let's examine how we can insert some rows into our students table:

```
mysql>insert into students
(studentid, studentlastname, studentfirstname, studentmajor, studententry)
values(123445678, "Carson", "Cathy", "CPI", 01/06/2006), (234556789, "Moore", "Mike", "CTT",
08/06/2006);
Query OK, 2 rows affected (0.00 sec)
Records: 2 Duplicates: 0 Warnings 0
```

If your screen looks like this, you have successfully added two records to your database. We could add one row at a time or add multiple rows. MySQL supports both.

Perhaps we only have the studentid and their first and last names. We want to get them into the system and enter major and entry date in a later transaction. We can also do this with the insert statement. To do this we use the following command:

```
mysql>insert into students(studentid, studentlastname, studentfirstname)
values(089776543, "Simms", "Phil"), (345669876, "Franks", "Fran") ;
Query OK, 2 rows affected (0.00 sec)
Records: 2 Duplicates: 0 Warnings 0
```

In a future lesson we will learn how to update existing records to insert the missing values into these records. Once again, practice these commands and experiment with them so you understand how to use them in an application program.

Lesson 12.2 - Show Data in a Table

There are several commands that help the user discover what is hidden in the database. One is the "show" command and the other is the "select" command. We will cover the "select" command in more detail in a future lesson. To see what tables are available you need to use the "show tables" command. Show tables in our school database at this point will show:

```
mysql> show tables;

+-----------------------------------+
| Tables in school                  |
+-----------------------------------+
```

```
| students                           |
+-----------------------------------+
1 rows in set (0.00 sec)
```

To see the data in a table we need to use a select command. The select command in its simplest form where we select all columns and rows from a given table will be used. We will select all columns from the students table. The command should look something like this:

```
mysql> select * from students;
+-----------+----------------+-----------------+-------------+-------------+
| studentid | studentlastname | studentfirstname | studentmajor | studententry |
+-----------+----------------+-----------------+-------------+-------------+
| 123445678 | Carson         | Cathy           | CPI         | 01/06/2006  |
| 234556789 | Moore          | Mike            | CTT         | 08/06/2006  |
| 089776543 | Simms          | Phil            | CPI         | 07/13/2006  |
| 345669876 | Franks         | Fran            |             |             |
+-----------+----------------+-----------------+-------------+-------------+
4 rows in set (0.00 sec)
```

All four records in the students table are shown.

In an instance where you want to see only those students with a major of CPI you might use a select statement that looks like this:

```
mysql> select * from students where studentmajor = "CPI";
+-----------+----------------+-----------------+-------------+-------------+
| studentid | studentlastname | studentfirstname | studentmajor | studententry |
+-----------+----------------+-----------------+-------------+-------------+
| 123445678 | Carson         | Cathy           | CPI         | 01/06/2006  |
| 089776543 | Simms          | Phil            | CPI         | 07/13/2006  |
+-----------+----------------+-----------------+-------------+-------------+
2 rows in set (0.00 sec)
```

As you can see, the "where" clause specifies only those records with a studentmajor of "CPI" are to be selected and the resulting display shows only those two records with "CPI" in the studentmajor field.

Lesson 12.3 - Summary

This has been a brief introduction to some of the basics of SQL as it relates to MySQL. There may be some differences depending on the version of MySQL used but these should be minor and rare. You must get used to writing these statements from the command line as this knowledge will be necessary to write dynamic web sites using PHP. A hint in using the command line is that if you make a mistake, you can use the up arrow to get back to prior lines of typing, correct the line and then hit enter. This saves some typing frustrations. Lots of practice will help you understand the various statements. If you are having trouble with the statements there are tools such as phpMyAdmin that will allow you to do many of the tasks in a GUI and shows you the correct syntax to enter at the command line to do the same task.

In Review:

1. Use the _____ command to put data into a table.
    a.   use
    b.   create
    c.   input
    d.   insert

2. There are several commands that help the user discover what is hidden in a database. Which of the following is not one of these commands.

    a.   show
    b.   selections
    c.   item
    d.   all of the above.

3. In a select statement, the _____ clause specifies which records are to be retrieved.

    a.   where
    b.   when
    c.   from
    d.   order

Start Programming with PHP

An Introduction to PHP and MySQL

Lesson 13.0 – MySQL – SQL Data Manipulation

We continue on with our exploration of the MySQL Relational Database. We have covered creating databases, creating tables, adding data to the tables and several administrator commands. Now we will look at altering existing tables, updating existing records, deleting data, tables or even databases, and building queries to look at the data from different views.

Lesson 13.1 - Altering an Existing Table

Sometimes we need to change our data tables. In this lesson we will look at adding a field to an existing database table. This is done with the "alter table" command. The syntax for this command is:

> alter table *tablename* add *fieldname type modifiers*;

This command adds a new field to the table. There is also a command that modifies an existing field in a table. The syntax for this command is:

> alter table *tablename* modify *fieldname type modifiers*;

In our students table we want to add a field called "studentgrad" which will have a value of either yes or no to indicate whether a student has graduated or not. We will use the enum type to do this. The command and the resulting response would look something like this:

```
mysql> alter table students add studentgrad enum("Yes", "No");
Query OK, 4 rows affected (0.00 sec)
Records: 4 Duplicates: 0 Warnings: 0
```

Now we are able to modify existing tables by modifying the existing fields or adding new fields as required.

Lesson 13.2 - Updating Records

The next step is to learn how to change the data in existing records. Often we do not have all the information to build a complete record and go back at a later date to add the remaining data. Another scenario is that often there is a need to change data within a record. Lastly there are instances where we may want to change all records in the table. To accomplish these tasks we use one of two forms of the "update" command in SQL. The syntax of the update command to update all records is:

> update *tablename* set *fieldname = newvalue*;

If we want to update a particular record we use a different form of the update command.

> update *tablename* set *fieldname = newvalue* where *fieldname = value*;

We return to our students table to update those records that do not have a major or a entry date defined. We will build SQL statements to update those records with values. This is where SQL

114

gets a little tricky. We need to be sure we are updating the correct record(s). This is where it becomes evident that it is important to have a "unique" identifier for every record in a table. This is why we set the studentid field with the unique modifier so that we know we have a value we can search on that will return only one record. Making this field the primary key just makes this search faster when we do it. We can build these update commands from the command line or from a program. In our example here we will use the command line. So to give studentid = 089776543 a major of "CPI" and a entry date of 09/01/2006 we would issue the following command:

```
mysql> update students set studentmajor="CPI" where studentid=089776543;
Query OK, 1 row affected (0.00 sec)
mysql> update students set studententry=09/01/2006 where studentid=089776543;
Query OK, 1 row affected (0.00 sec)
```

We have now updated the record for studentid = 098776543 with a major and entry date. To update the other record we go back to the command line and issue the following commands:

```
mysql> update students set studentmajor="CHH" where studentid=345669876;
Query OK, 1 row affected (0.00 sec)
mysql> update students set studententry=09/01/2006 where studentid=345669876;
Query OK, 1 row affected (0.00 sec)
```

Not very efficient for the human interface but this is generally done by a GUI interface in Microsoft Access and OpenOffice.org Base or a myriad of other GUI interfaces for relational databases. We can also use the power of SQL in our application programs where the program generates the commands and executes them.

Lesson 13.3 - Deleting Data, Tables & Databases

Data, Fields, Tables and Databases can be deleted by MySQL commands. I do not recommend that you do any of these commands until you have a good understanding of MySQL and how commands and queries work in general. You can do unrepairable damage to your database with these commands and therefore I am just going to review the syntax without giving you examples to try in your MySQL database. If you are interested in attempting these commands, I recommend that you build a simple database and use that for this type of experimentation.

To delete a specific record from a table you use the "delete from" command. The syntax for this command is:

delete from *tablename* where *fieldname* = *value*;

To delete a field from a table you can use the "alter table" SQL command. The syntax for this command is:

alter table *tablename* drop *fieldname*;

You can delete a complete table using the "drop table" SQL command. The syntax for this command is:

drop table *tablename*;

An entire database can be deleted using the "drop database" SQL command. The syntax for this command is:

drop database *databasename*;

As you can immagine, a lot of damage can be done with one of these commands. Once the command has executed there is no way to retrieve the data lost. Only if you have the foresight to backup your database prior to the delete can you retrieve the information. This is why some of the more robust industrial strength database products have a built in mechanism to help the administrator should this occur. Usually only the database administrators have this power or this is done by a computer application program. Rarely is this left to the individual user to do these deletes. Even as an administrator function, some databases use a single commit or a double commit to make these commands less likely to be executed by accident. Single commit is requiring the administrator to issue a second command, the "commit" command before the item is actually deleted. In a double commit the administrator is asked a second time to confirm the delete with another commit command.

We now move on to what may be the most important command set in the SQL programming language. The commands that allow you to access the data stored in tables.

Lesson 13.4 - Building Queries in MySQL

The "select" command is perhaps the one command that runs from the simplest command to the most complicated command. It is essential to finding the information stored in your tables. Therefore it may be one of the most valualble SQL commands and needs to be understood by anyone using SQL databases. In many ways you are doing something very similar to what you do when you do a Google search or a search in any other search engine. Yes, they too are databases and the search criteria you enter for your search is really some information that is used in a select command for the particular database you are searching.

The most basic form of the select command is:

```
select * from tablename;
```

This selects all columns and all rows from the named table. If there are 100 rows in the table, you get all 100 rows. Running this command against our students file would result in the following:

```
mysql> select * from students;

+-----------+----------------+-----------------+------------+------------+----------+
|studentid  |studentlastname |studentfirstname |studentmajor|studententry|studentgrad|
+-----------+----------------+-----------------+------------+------------+----------+
| 123445678 | Carson         | Cathy           | CPI        | 01/06/2006 | No       |
| 234556789 | Moore          | Mike            | CTT        | 08/06/2006 | NO       |
| 089776543 | Simms          | Phil            | CPI        | 09/01/2006 | NO       |
| 345669876 | Franks         | Fran            | CHH        | 09/01/2006 | NO       |
+-----------+----------------+-----------------+------------+------------+----------+
4 rows in set (0.00 sec)
```

It is not always the case that we want to see all rows and columns. This is the real power of SQL. We can construct a select statement that will present only the columns and rows required for a specific task or operation. The general syntax of the select statement is:

> select *columns list* from *tableslist* ... *additional options*;

In the "columns list" you specify the columns you wish to select, in the "tableslist" you select the table or multiple tables that contain the data you wish to select. In the "additional information" is where you give directions to the database engine on the "rules" to use in selecting and presenting the data back to the requestor. This is the critical part of the select statement.

116

The first clause we will look at is probably the most important. The "where" clause tells the database engine how to find the columns in the rows given. It is the basic rules for accessing the information. The syntax is:

select *columns list* from *tableslist* where *selection rules*;

Let's look at some sample queries using a single table. First we will select all studentlastname entries from the students table:

```
mysql> select studentlastname from students;

+------------------+
| studentlastname  |
+------------------+
| Carson           |
| Moore            |
| Simms            |
| Franks           |
+------------------+
4 rows in set (0.00 sec)
```

This gives us every row in the table because we have not specified any rules for selection. So, let's give some rules using the where clause. We want to select the first and last names of all students with a major of "CPI". So the select statement and results would be:

```
mysql> select studentfirstname, studentlastname, studentmajor from students where
studentmajor="CPI";

+------------------+--------------------+---------------------+
| studentfirsname  | studentlastname    | studentmajor        |
+------------------+--------------------+---------------------+
| Carson           | Cathy              | CPI                 |
| Simms            | Phil               | CPI                 |
+------------------+--------------------+---------------------+
2 rows in set (0.00 sec)
```

The last example we will do will require 2 tables. You need to create a majors table with two fields (1) major that will match with the studentmajor field in the students table and (2) a majordesc field that will hold the description. Then you will put an entries into the table for: major CPI majordesc Programming & Internet; CTT Computer Science Transfer; CPI Programming and Internet; and CHH Hardware and Help Desk

The point here goes to the relational nature of the tables in a database. You must have relationships between tables to allow the joining of the table information in the queries you set up in application or request processing. This is where you find out if you have successfully "normalized" your tables. Quite often you will find that you have not provided the proper relationships between tables to allow you to do some requests for data that you will need to do in your application. This may be just adding a field or worst case redesign of the database. This is where careful planning is ESSENTIAL in developing your database and having a Entity Relationship Diagram (ERD) that is complete, accurate and well planned.

Back to our example. Lets select studentid, studentlastname, studentmajor and majordescr from the students and majors tables. Our request and results should look something like this:

```
mysql> select studentid, studentlastname, studentmajor, majordescr from students,
majors where studentmajor = major;
```

117

```
+--------------+----------------------+---------------+----------------------------+
| studentid    | studentlastname      | studentmajor  | majordescr                 |
+--------------+----------------------+---------------+----------------------------+
| 123445678    | Carson               | CPI           | Programming & Internet     |
| 234556789    | Moore                | CTT           | Computer Science Transfer  |
| 089776543    | Simms                | CPI           | Programming & Internet     |
| 345669876    | Franks               | CHH           | Hardware Help Desk         |
+--------------+----------------------+---------------+----------------------------+
```

There are many more ways to use the "select" statement but we will leave that for future lessons. This should give you enough to get started using your databases. We have covered most of the fundamentals and now it is time for you to practice these commands and then move on and explore additional SQL capabilities.

Lesson 13.5 - Summary

This chapter introduced some of the other commands available in MySQL. At this point you should have a good understanding of how to use MySQL and its SQL commands from the command line. As I said before, knowing how to construct various SQL commands will help later when you write PHP programs to control SQL databases and HTML.

In Review:

1. To add a field named "pay" to a data table named "emp" use the command.
   a.   `alter table emp add pay;`
   b.   `alter pay add to emp;`
   c.   `add pay to emp;`
   d.   `select emp add pay;`
2. To change the value of the "pay" field to 10.00, in the table "emp" for the row with the empid field with a value of 123.
   a.   `change pay to 10.00 table emp empid = 123;`
   b.   `update pay = 10.00 in table emp where empid = 123;`
   c.   `update emp set pay = 10.00 where empid = 123;`
   d.   `update emp pay=10.00 where empid = 123;`
3. Delete all items from the table emp where the value of the pay field is greater than 100.00.
   a.   `drop emp for all fields > 100.00;`
   b.   `delete emp for all fields > 100.00;`
   c.   `drop from emp where pay > 100.00;`
   d.   `delete from emp where pay > 100.00;`
4. To delete an entire database named emp use:
   a.   `delete database emp;`
   b.   `drop database emp;`
   c.   `delete emp;`
   d.   `drop emp;`
5. The select command that displays all rows and all columns of a database table named emp.
   a.   `select all from emp;`
   b.   `show all from emp;`
   c.   `select * from emp;`
   d.   `show * from emp;`

Start Programming with PHP

An Introduction to PHP and MySQL

LESSON 14: PHP and MySQL

This lesson concentrates on connecting to a MySQL database from a PHP program. This is a commonly used process for PHP programs when retrieving data from a database or writing data to a database in online programs.

Lesson14-1 Connect to a MySQL Database

Before a database can be created or accessed in any way the program must connect to MySQL. The mysql_connect function handles this connection and because these examples were done in server2go the first parameter for the function is "localhost". In our example we have assigned the username "root" to a variable named $user and use the variable name to connect to MySQL in the second parameter. At this point the root user does not have a password as indicated by the "" as the third parameter in the connect statement. If all works we will display a message in a web page titled "Connect to MySQL". The message "You have connected to MySQL" indicates a successful connection.

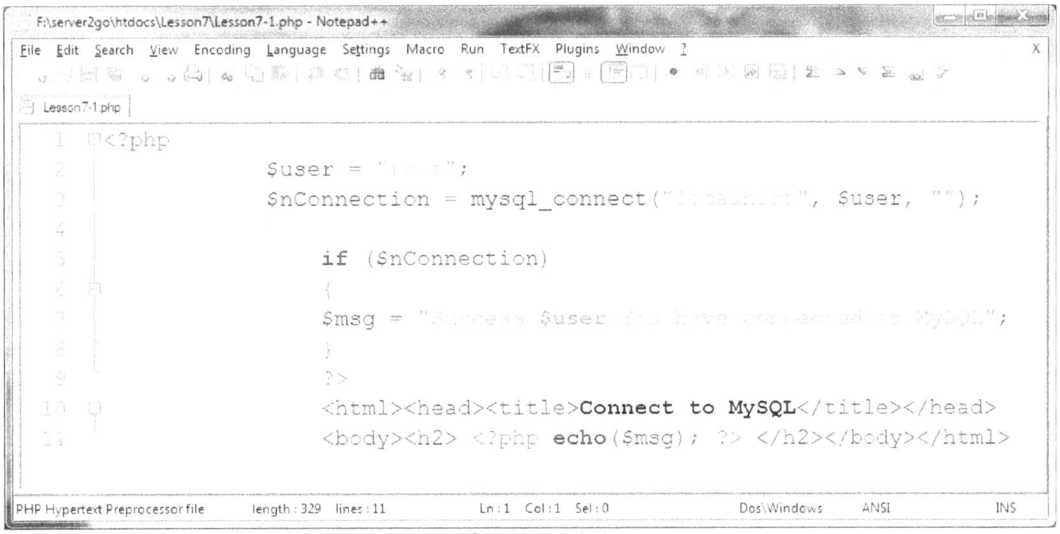

Figure 14.1.1

Figure 14.1.2

As indicated above, the code to connect to MySQL worked.

Lesson14-2 - What databases are available in MySQL?

In this example we connect to MySQL as in the last lesson but add a line that begins with the or die() function. If the connection to MySQL fails the or die() function is executed which displays the message between the parenthesis "You did not connect to MySQL" and terminates the program. If the connection is successful the mysql_list_dba() function builds a list of the available databases and displays them in the default browser in the web page at the end of the program.

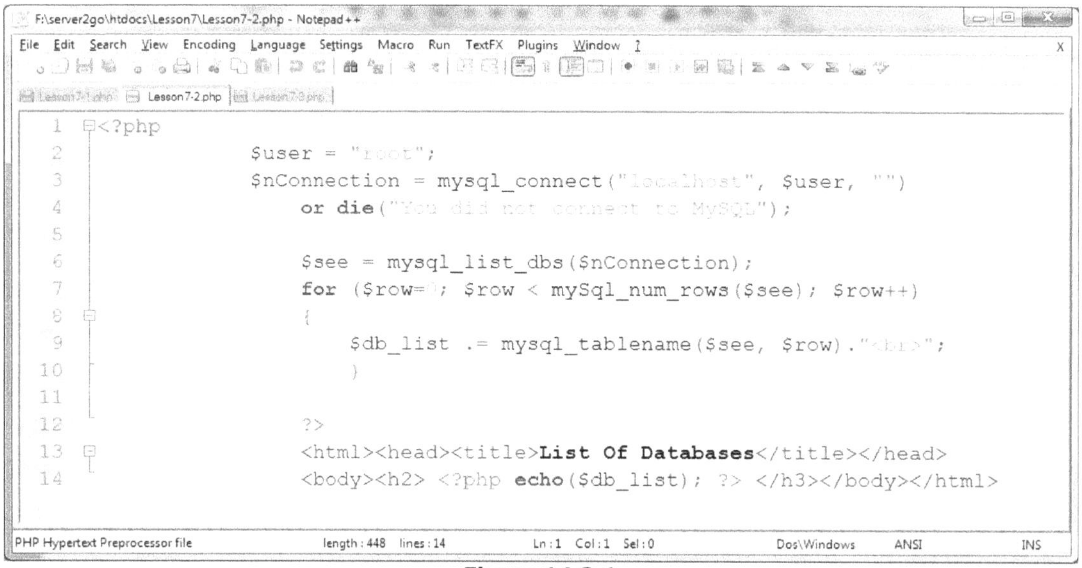

Figure 14.2.1

The program connects to MySQL and if successful, prints a list of the databases available in the current MySQL database. (See Figure 14.2.2)

Figure 14.2.2

The resulting display indicates the presence of six databases in this instance of MySQL. Some have been created by the installation of MySQL, phpMyAdmin and the remainder by users.

information_schema
mysql
phpmyadmin
server2go

120

The above databases were created by the installation of various products and should not be removed.

Lesson14-3 - Show the databases and the tables.

If the connection is successful PHP uses the mysql_tablename and mysql_list_dba to build a list of the databases and the underlying tables within the database. The output is shown in the default browser using the HTML code supplied.

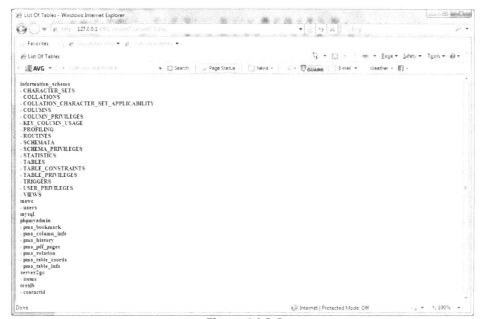

Figure 14.3.1

The next figure shows the databases in MySQL as well as the tables that are members of each database.

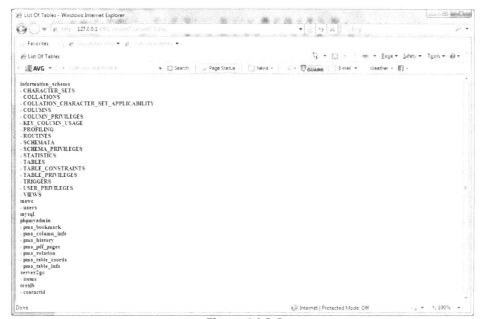

Figure 14.3.2

121

The top part of the listing with database tables under Information_schema are all in upper case letters, these are system tables and should not be changed or deleted.

Lesson14-4 - Create a New Database

If the connection to MySQL is successful, we issue the SQL command "CREATE DATABASE my_new_db" if it already exists the message "Error: database not created:" will be displayed. If it does not exist it will be created and the message "Database my_new_db" will be displayed.

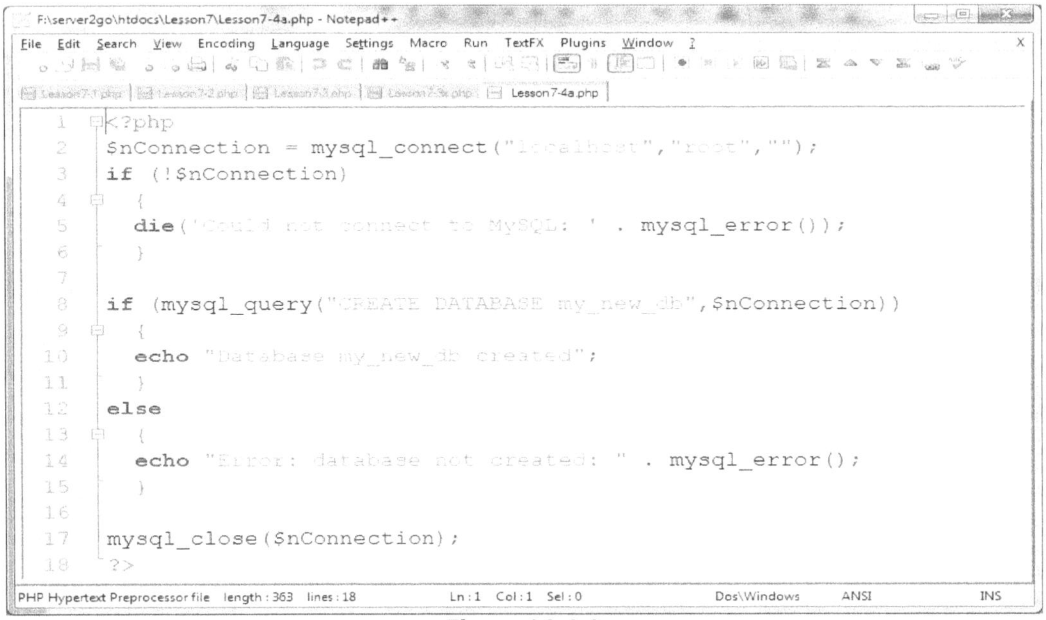

```
<?php
$nConnection = mysql_connect("localhost","root","");
if (!$nConnection)
  {
  die('Could not connect to MySQL: ' . mysql_error());
  }

if (mysql_query("CREATE DATABASE my_new_db",$nConnection))
  {
  echo "Database my_new_db created";
  }
else
  {
  echo "Error: database not created: " . mysql_error();
  }

mysql_close($nConnection);
?>
```

Figure 14.4.1

REPEAT Lesson14-2. PHP program written to confirm databases existing in the MySQL installation.

Lesson14-5 - Create a New Table

After connecting to MySQL, we attempt to create the database my_new_db and if it does not exist (has not been created) it will be created and the message "Database created" will be displayed. If the database my_new_db exists (has been created) the message "Error creating database" will be displayed and the new table will be created.

The SQL command "`CREATE TABLE Friends`" creates the new table named Friends and the four fields in the table created.

No data has been stored in the table to this point.

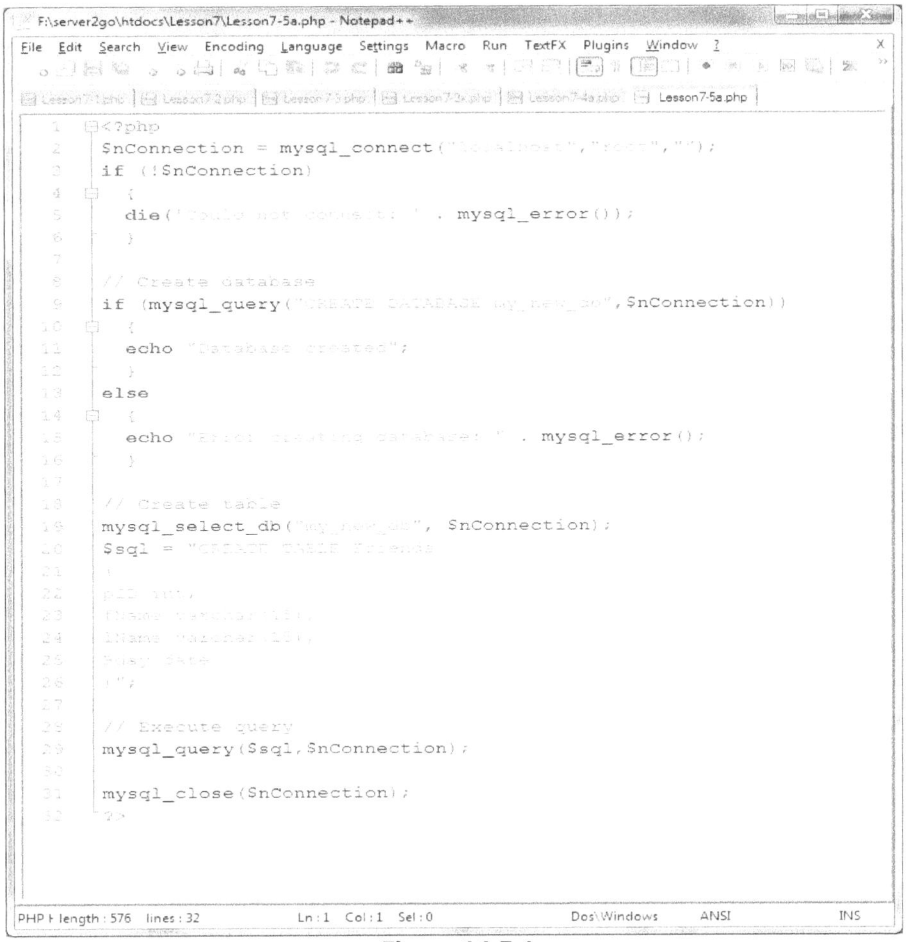

F:\server2go\htdocs\Lesson7\Lesson7-5a.php - Notepad++

```
<?php
$nConnection = mysql_connect([illegible]);
if (!$nConnection)
  {
  die([illegible] . mysql_error());
  }

// Create database
if (mysql_query([illegible],$nConnection))
  {
  echo "Database created";
  }
else
  {
  echo [illegible] . mysql_error();
  }

// Create table
mysql_select_db([illegible], $nConnection);
$sql = [illegible]
[illegible]
[illegible]
[illegible]
[illegible]
[illegible]
[illegible]

// Execute query
mysql_query($sql,$nConnection);

mysql_close($nConnection);
?>
```

PHP length : 576 lines : 32 Ln : 1 Col : 1 Sel : 0 Dos\Windows ANSI INS

Figure 14.5.1

Confirm the creation of the table named Friends in the my_new_db database by running the program created in Lesson 14-3.

Lesson14-6 - Put Data in the New Table

This php program opens MySQL and selects the database my_new_db. Then inserts two records into the Friends table and closes the MySQL session. Note there is NO output for this program.

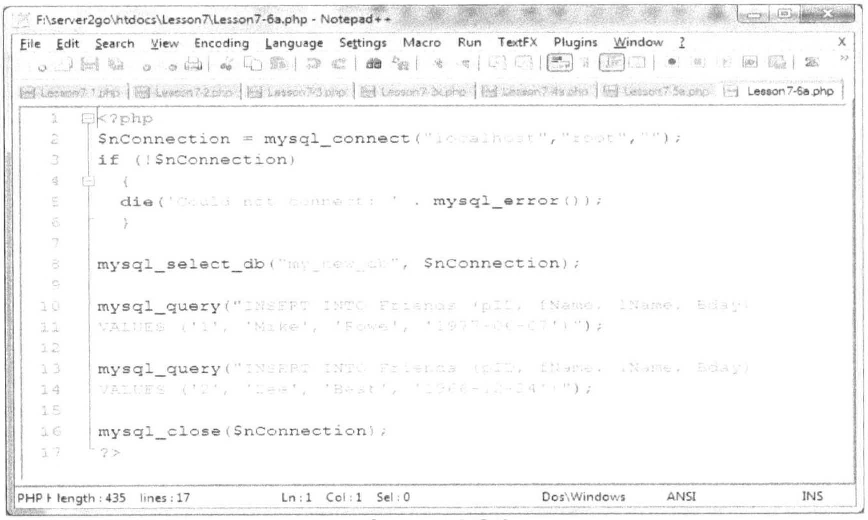

Figure 14.6.1

We now have two rows of data in the Friends table. This can be confirmed by the material covered in the next lesson. The data may also be viewed using one of the Administrative tools like phpMyAdmin (covered in Lesson 16).

Note that the lines 10 through 14 are SQL commands. The INSERT INTO Friends.... is the SQL statement that place a new row into the database currently open named my_new_db. The PHP function mysql_query() takes the SQL statement and executes it in the MySQL system. The SQL statement is the same SQL statement that would be typed at the command line if the query was being run from the command-line.

It is important that the mysql_close() function is executed. This insures that the data from the last SQL statement executed is written to the database.

Lesson14-7 - Display the Data in the Table in an HTML Table

This PHP program opens MySQL and selects the my_new_db database and selects all rows in the Friends table. The difference here is that this PHP program is embedded in an HTML document in the body section.

124

Figure 14.7.1

The PHP program embedded in the HTML builds a table. The table has a border of 1 pixel. It has a title row followed by a row constructed for each row in the Friends table. This will build a table that will hold as many rows as necessary to display all of the rows resulting from the select statement.

Figure 14.7.2

As you see, the two rows inserted in the prior step are displayed in a table with five columns, each with an appropriate heading.

Lesson 14-8 – Summary

This lesson showed how to connect to MySQL from a PHP program. How to create a new database, create tables and insert data into those tables. It also demonstrated how to see the databases and their respective tables within the MySQL installation.

In Review:

1. The _____ function establishes the connection between PHP and MySQL.
    - a.   mysql_connect()
    - b.   connect_mysql()
    - c.   my_sql_connect()
    - d.   connect()
2. If the connection to MySQL fails, the _____ function is used to provide an error routine.
    - a.   try()
    - b.   catch()
    - c.   error()
    - d.   die()
3. If the connection to MySQL is successful, the _____ function builds a list of the available databases.
    - a.   list_dba()
    - b.   mysql_list_dba()
    - c.   mysql_dba()
    - d.   dba_mysql()

Start Programming with PHP

An Introduction to PHP and MySQL

LESSON 15: Coding a PHP Form Application

USING PHP TO GENERATE A FORM WITH A RESPONSE:

Lesson 15-1 Generating Code Files

This is a lesson that uses a group of PHP programs and files to put a form on the screen that asks several questions. When the form is submitted a php program builds a form that echos back the responses to the various questions on the form. They also illustrate a couple of other PHP programming techniques.

First, note how in the index.php, the php scripts are scattered through the HTML file. The index file has the extension of .php not .html. The very first script is just used to generate the first few HTML instructions. This script addressing a text file may be used by many different files. Any time there is HTML code common to multiple PHP programs, this technique is used.

It illustrates the use of random numbers. Generating a style for the page is shown. Then a php script within heading tags. Next a script that puts the contents of a text file on the HTML page.

The last script in index.php shows the script reading the system date, extracting the day of the week and then displaying a message based on a comparison of the value returned using an if statement.

Let's pick apart our first PHP program.

INDEX.PHP

```php
<?php
include("startpage.txt");
?>
<?php
$ir = rand(150, 255);
$ig = rand(150, 255);
$ib = rand(150, 255);
$srgb = "background-color: rgb(" . $ir . "," . $ig . "," .  $ib . ")";
// echo $srgb;
?>
</head>
<body style = "<?php echo $srgb ?>" >
    <h1>Dunes 'n Grass<?php echo" -- Surfs Up -- " ?></h1>
    <p>
    <form action = "result.php" method = "GET" >
        What is your favorite color? <input type="text" name = "color" />
<br />
        What is your age? <input type="text" name = "age" /> <br />
        What is your password? <input type="password" name = "pwd" /> <br />
        <input type="submit" value = "do it!" />
    </form>
    </p>
```

127

```
        <p>
        Here we learn to teach from the beach!
        <br />PHP on the sand at Ocean City?
        <br />MySQL on Fenwick Island.
        </p>
        <p>
            <pre>
        <?php include("quote.txt"); ?>
            </pre>
        </p>
        <p>
        <?php
$d=date("D");
if ($d=="Wed")
  echo "See You Thursday!";
else
  echo "Have a nice day!";
?>
        </p>
</body>
</html>
```

Break apart the program into it's components. Look at the PHP code, look at the HTML code.

```
<?php
include("startpage.txt");
?>
```

This first PHP script includes the contents of a text file named "startpage.txt". This is a text file that contains the top part of our HTML document.

```
<?php
$ir = rand(150, 255);
$ig = rand(150, 255);
$ib = rand(150, 255);

$srgb = "background-color: rgb(" . $ir . "," . $ig . "," .  $ib . ")";
// echo $srgb;
?>
```

The next PHP script creates 3 random numbers between 150 and 255. These random numbers will be used to determine the background-color of the web page. $ir is for the red value, $ig for the green value and $ib for the blue value to be used to build the RGB values for the background-color attribute. We exclude the values between 0 and 149 as they would generate very dark colors. Remember, this combination of colors could produce black on black as our font color will be black.

```
</head>
<body style = "<?php echo $srgb ?>" >
```

This PHP script uses the background-color we set in the head phase.

```
        <h1>Dunes 'n Grass<?php echo" -- Surfs Up -- " ?></h1>
```

This PHP script echos a string literal within a set of h1 tags.

128

```
        <p>
        <form action = "result.php" method = "GET" >
                What is your favorite color? <input type="text" name = "color" />
<br />
                What is your age? <input type="text" name = "age" /> <br />
                What is your password? <input type="password" name = "pwd" /> <br />
                <input type="submit" value = "do it!" />
        </form>
        </p>
        <p>
        Here we learn to teach from the beach!   <br />PHP on the sand at Ocean City?
<br />MySQL on the beach in Fenwick Island.
        </p>
        <p>
                <pre>
        <?php include("quote.txt"); ?>
```

This PHP script is set between preformat tags. This will print out the contents of a text file named "quote.txt".

```
                </pre>
        </p>
        <p>


        <?php
$d=date("D");
if ($d=="Wed")
   echo "See You Thursday!";
else
   echo "Have a nice day!";
?>
```

This PHP script gathers the day from the system date into a variable named $d. Then the contents of $d is compared to the string literal "Wed". If equal prints a message "See You Thursday!", if NOT equal it prints "Have a nice day!" to the screen.

```
        </p>
</body>
</html>
```

The last three lines are the ending to the HTML code, wrapping up with the closing tags for the body and the html file.

STARTPAGE.TXT

The second is a text file that generates the first five lines of any HTML page. First a script the outputs the DOCTYPE for an XHTML program. Then the first four lines of an HTML page.

```
<?php
echo"<!DOCTYPE html PUBLIC \"-//W3C//DTD XHTML
1.1//EN\" \"http://www.w3.org/TR/xhtml11/DTD/xhtml11.dtd\">";
?>
<html>
<head>
```

129

```
        <title>MAWCC PHP Prototype </title>
        <meta http-equiv="content-type" content="application/xhtml+xml; charset=UTF-
8" />
```

Break apart this code into its PHP and HTML code.

```
<?php
echo"<!DOCTYPE html PUBLIC \"-//W3C//DTD XHTML
1.1//EN\" \"http://www.w3.org/TR/xhtml11/DTD/xhtml11.dtd\">";
?>
```

This PHP script creates an XHTML header.

```
<html>
<head>
        <title>Sample PHP Prototype </title>
        <meta http-equiv="content-type" content="application/xhtml+xml; charset=UTF-
8" />
```

QUOTE.TXT

This is a text file that will be displayed in the body of the HTML page.

```
Weeks of programming can save hours of planning!
```

The contents of a text file to be displayed within the web page.

RESULT.PHP

The last PHP program uses the startpage.php.

```
<?php
include("startpage.txt");
?>

</head>
<body>
        <h1>FORM RESULTS</h1>
        <p>
        <?php
        $scolor = $_GET["color"];
        $iage = $_GET["age"];
        $ipwd = $_GET["pwd"];
        // $sRGB = $_GET["srgb"];
        echo "Your favorite color is " . $scolor;
        echo "<br />Your age is ";
        echo $iage;
        echo "<br />Your Password ";
        echo $ipwd;
        ?>
        </p>
```

```
        <?php
$d=date("D");
if ($d=="Wed")
  echo "See You Thursday!";
else
  echo "Have a nice day!";
?>
        </p>
</body>
</html>
```

The analysis of this code is as follows:

```
<?php
include("startpage.txt");
?>
```

This first PHP script includes the contents of a text file named "startpage.txt". This is a text file that contains the top part of our HTML document. The next script retrieves the data sent from the form and puts it in variables. The contents of the variables is then used to generate a response page repeating the data entered into the form.

```
</head>
<body>
        <h1>FORM RESULTS</h1>
        <p>

        <?php
        $scolor = $_GET["color"];
        $iage = $_GET["age"];
        $ipwd = $_GET["pwd"];
        // $sRGB = $_GET["srgb"];
        echo "Your favorite color is " . $scolor;
        echo "<br />Your age is ";
        echo $iage;
        echo "<br />Your Password ";
        echo $ipwd;
        ?>
```

This PHP script generates the values returned from the submitted form. It gets the values from what was submitted, taking them from the system variables where the submitted values were stored. Favorite color was stored in "color", Age was stored in "age" and the Password was stored in "pwd". The script gets each value and stores it in a variable. The variable is then used to build output to the reply screen being generated.

```
        </p>
        <?php
$d=date("D");
if ($d=="Wed")
  echo "See You Thursday!";
else
  echo "Have a nice day!";
?>
```

This PHP script gathers the day from the system date into a variable named $d. Then the

131

contents of $d is compared to the string literal "Wed". If equal prints a message "See You Thursday!", if NOT equal it prints "Have a nice day!" to the screen.

```
      </p>
</body>
</html>
```

Lesson 15-2 USING WHAT YOU HAVE LEARNED:

Your challenge is to put these files into a working web site. Once that has been done, make modifications to the files to make it do another task. Ask different questions, format the reply screen differently. Use different dates or comparison criteria. Different look and feel for all pages.

This is your chance to modify some existing code and experiment with various commands and parameters to understand how they work.

Lesson 15-3 SUMMARY:

PHP can generate dynamic web pages. This exercise illustrates many of the techniques that can be used. Once again planning your approach to the problem solution can be a big advantage when generating your code. Code used repeatedly in several pages can be placed in a separate file and included each time it is required. Review this code carefully, implement it and then play with the code to make it do other things. Practice is the best way to learn.

In Review:

1. Enter the programs in this lesson and get them working. Then, start making changes to the various programs to create your own new programs. The trial and error of making changes will be helpful in understanding the process for future programs.

Start Programming with PHP

An Introduction to PHP and MySQL

Lesson 16 – MySQL GUI and Report Writers

Lesson 16.0 - GUI for MySQL

MySQL is not Microsoft Access, a database wrapped in a cute GUI to make everything happen with a point and a click. No, MySQL can only offer a command line interface and who likes to use that. Unfortunately we are all spoiled by the nice GUI interface of Microsoft Access and the plain GUI interface of products like OpenOffice.org Base. So, how do we get a nice GUI interface that helps us harness the power of the MySQL database product?

Short and sweet, we download one or we purchase a commercial product. Just a quick Google search turned up a few products. Of course, the most obvious and most selected is phpMyAdmin. This seems to be the product of choice for MySQL. Some of the others I encountered were:

* PHPMyAdmin
* Adminer
* Navicat
* Dreamcoder
* AnySQL Maestro
* EMS SQL Manager for MySQL 4.5
* SQLiteManager

Lesson 16.1 - Advantages / Disadvantages

Getting tied to a GUI interface has some advantages and some disadvantages. These advantages and disadvantages seem to change according to how we look at them, from the learning viewpoint or from the production viewpoint. It is definitely advantageous to learn MySQL from the command line but you loose productivity which makes it not as valuable for someone who needs to get the job done and time is money. Students like to take this short cut but they don't learn the SQL skills necessary to go to the next step which is writing code for web based database sites.

ADVANTAGES:
* Rapid development of database objects.
* Easier data entry.
* Easy to update data
* You do not need to know SQL commands.
* Shows SQL commands for each operation.

DISADVANTAGES
* Does not replace knowing SQL commands when writing PHP programs.
* May not be available on all platforms.
* May not be available for all versions of MySQL.
* Not knowing SQL commands may hinder debugging or problem solving.

The GUI we will study in this course is phpMyAdmin is the best and most used GUI interface that is free, that is currently available. It is widely documented so it is the obvious choice. Others may offer features that are good for special requirements, but phpMyAdmin seems to be preferred

133

by most developers. So, we begin our study of various products with an overview of phpMyAdmin.

Lesson 16.2 - phpMyAdmin

Perhaps, the most used of all the tools, PHPMyAdmin is a GUI interface to assist in the management of MySQL databases. This is a free download and is included in downloads like WampServer, XAMPP, and server2go.
- Requirements:
- PHP 4.0 or later
- MySQL 3.32.32 or later
- Any Web Browser with cookies enabled.

PHPMyAdmin was designed to reduce time to administer MySQL databases and ease in creating new databases and tables. A better alternative to using the MySQL commands from the command line.

The installation of PHPMyAdmin is fairly simple and is well documented. Once installed, you can start creating and managing databases with PHPMyAdmin.

To create a new database, look on the right side of the PHPMyAdmin control panel and you will see an area that says **Create a new database**. Just enter the name of the database you wish to create. When the process is complete, you will see a success message along with the SQL command used to create this database. Everything you do in PHPMyAdmin it will show you the SQL commands it has used. This is a great way to learn more about the SQL command set.

Then you will see a message at the bottom that reminds you that your database does not have any tables to store data. It displays a dialog box that will allow you to create a table. You should create your first table at this point.

PHPMyAdmin then moves to another   page that will allow you to create and define the fields required in your table. You may then go on to create the remainder of the tables that you need to complete your database.

Now you are ready to insert data. Perhaps the data will come from entry using PHPMyAdmin or from other web applications that already exist or are yet to be written.

Lesson 16.3 – GUI Product Analysis

Let's look at a brief overview of each of the other products listed above.

Adminer
This is a small php program that will give you some big program results. Another great free product. You can even customize it with various CSS files for the application.

Dreamcoder
Provides a convenient interface that makes the database administrator more productive. You can create, edit, duplicate, export and delete objects.   Compile and run stored procedures. Export and import data, generate reports, monitor the database activity. Synchronize the database, build and execute queries, format code, create users and execute scripts.

AnySQL Maestro
A multipurpose administration tool for database management, control and development. It

134

supports a number of databases including MySQL. It features a database designer, data management (editing, grouping, sorting and filtering), a SQL editor, and a query builder. It will also export/import to/from the most popular formats. Exists in both a Freeware and a Professional version.

EMS SQL Manager for MySQL 4.5
A high performance tool to manage MySQL databases. It supports all versions of MySQL and all features of these versions. It uses wizards to assist new users in creating databases or managing existing databases. It is labeled as shareware and costs $175.00 to purchase.

SQLiteManager
A minimum function SQL manager that is provided with some versions of Wampserver.

Lesson 16.4 - Report Builders

Having data stored in a database is no good unless you can see that data. We can all agree that we can see it from the command line or from the other tools we have discussed but it is not pretty. Users like pretty little reports.

Navicat
Used to build custom reports. Turns your data into valuable information. Helps build reports easily and can schedule them to run automatically on a predetermined schedule. Using the Report Viewer it allows multiple users to access reports anytime and anywhere. It will also build reports from Access, Excel,XML, PostgreSQL, Oracle and many other similar applications.

Crystal Reports
Crystal Reports is one of the leading commercial report generators. It is widely used by Microsoft products for report generation for the .NET products. It supports many types of databases and is an extremely flexible product.

JasperforMySQL
This product is exclusively for MySQL. Provides rich reporting for MySQL database information. It is a powerful and affordable product and has embeddable capabilities. Some of the key features are: Ad hoc reporting; Flexible report output in PDF, HTML, XML, Excel, RTF formats; Report scheduling and distribution; Language support; May be embedded in other software applications; Open XML-based report definitions.

PHP Report Maker
"CREATE DYNAMIC WEB REPORTS IN MINUTES! - PHP Report Maker is a powerful reporting tool that can generate dynamic PHP Web reports from MySQL databases. You can instantly create live detail and summary reports or crosstab reports for your Website. Flash charting (column, bar, line, pie, area, doughnut, multi-series, and stacked charts) is also supported. PHP Report Maker is designed for high flexibility, numerous options enable you to generate reports that best suit your needs. The generated codes are clean and easy-to-customize. PHP Report Maker can save you tons of time and is suitable for both beginners and experienced developers alike."
www.hkvstore.com/phpreportmaker

DataVision
"DataVision is a reporting tool similar to Crystal Reports. DV supports many data sources (JDBC, files) and many output formats (HTML, XML, PDF, LaTeX, Excel, delimited files, DocBook). DV includes a GUI Editor. DV is embeddable. Reports are XML based." datavision/sourceforge.net

Lesson 16.5 - Summary

First, this is only an overview of a rather large topic. There are many other products out there that could be included in this study. If you are investigating this type of product for a business, it bears further investigation. I strongly recommend that you download several of the freeware or shareware products and play with them. This is the best way for you to decide what products are capable of doing and my help you find a more cost effective solution for your business.

While I often recommend Open Source products and freeware products, they are not always the best fit for a given situation. You need to make an informed decision. Test with those products and if they fall short, you may often get a trial of a commercial product. If that gives you better results, then it is the best decision. If the results are equal or inferior, then go back to the Open Source or freeware product.

In Review:

1. Which is not an advantage of a GUI database interface.
    - a.   Easy data entry.
    - b.   Easy data update.
    - c.   Automatic normalization
    - d.   You do not need to know SQL commands
2. A popular free MySQL GUI interface.
    - a.   phpMyAdmin
    - b.   SQLiteManager
    - c.   Adminer
    - d.   All of the above
3. _____ is one of the leading commercial Report Generators.
    - a.   Navicat
    - b.   Dreamcoder
    - c.   QuikReport
    - d.   Crystal Reports

Start Programming with PHP

An Introduction to PHP and MySQL

Lesson 17 – Web Based Databases

The Web consists of computers on the Internet that are interconnected in a specific way, that makes computers and their contents easily accessible to each other. The Web has a client/server architecture which means that programs on servers communicate and share files with client workstations over a network.

You can create data-based Web pages using data that is retrieved from a database and then placed in the Web page. You can use either server-side processing or client-side processing to retrieve the data.

The client/server in web based databases, displays data in the following manner:

- User makes a request through the browser.
- Browser sends the request to the appropriate server.
- Server program generates a SQL query.
- Query is sent to the database engine.
- Database engine creates the correct response to the query.
- Response is sent back to the program on the server.
- Program generates the appropriate page or pages.
- Pages are returned to the browser.
- Browser displays to the user.

It sounds complicated and should take a while to process. But, this is exactly what Google, Amazon, Ebay and many other sites do many thousands or millions of times each day. Do they take a long time to run? No, if they did, nobody would use them. Done correctly, this is a very efficient process. But, you need to know an appropriate programming language and how to generate SQL statements.

Lesson 17.1 – Client Server

In client/server processing, part of the processing takes place on the client and part takes place on the server. When a database is accessed over the internet, the client computer requests information by completing a form on a web page which is sent to a program at the server which looks at the request, processes it and returns the results to the client computer in a format readable by the browser.

You can use many different technologies to create programs that generate data-based Web pages. These technologies differ based on whether the programs run on the server or on the client workstation, and whether the progams are stored in a text (script) format or in a machine language (compiled) format. The technologies are similar because all of them enable the user to interact with a database using his or her browser.

Lesson 17.2 – Programming Languages

There are many programming languages that may be used for accessing web based databases. Most of these are open source and supported by most browsers.

Perl – originally referred to as the "Duct Tape of the Internet".

PHP – teamed up with MySQL, is one of the most widely used and powerful combinations of programming language and database manager available for use for internet applications. Best of all, both are free.

JavaScript – not to be confused, in any way, with the JAVA programming language. This programming language is supported by most browsers. JavaScript can be embedded in HTML to provide a higher level of interactivity than is supported by HTML commands only.

JAVA – An object oriented language developed and supported by Sun Microsystems. Used in the web development field to create and use Java Applets.

AJAX – Originated in 2005 to assist in web development. Asynchronous JavaScript and XML (AJAX) is becoming another tool that makes programming for client side much easier than other languages and provides faster access to server side resources. A good example of the use of AJAX is in Google. When you begin to type in your search words, Google returns other search combinations based on what you are typing. You can select one of these and eliminate keystrokes or see what others are entering looking for similar resources.

Ruby – a relatively new, and billed as easy to use language often used with "Rails" hence the name "Ruby on Rails" makes the interface with web servers and server-side databases easier to program.

ASP.NET – a web development environment built on the Microsoft Common Runtime Language (CLR) used to build powerful web applications. The actual programming language can ba any of the 50+ dotNET supported languages including Visual Basic, Visual C# and Visual C++ from Microsoft.

Others – VBScript, J#, C#, C, C++, Python as well as numerous others. Most offer something unique in the programming, ease of use, interface capabilities or speed and availablilty.

Which one should you use? They are all tools to accomplish very similar tasks. So, it probably depends on many different factors including the task at hand, the knowledge of the programmer, the tools available to the programmer and perhaps the perception of free programming languages versus the commercial programming languages.

Lesson 17.3 – PHP/MySQL

One of the best sources of training for PHP and MySQL and using them together in web development is on the web site http://www.w3schools.com. This site is an excellent source of training for all web related topics. Keep this site bookmarked in **My Favorites** as this will be a useful source of future training if you decide to do web development. Your bookshelf of bookmarks can be your instant reference library that is always up to date.

Since this is a PHP course we will not go into any language other than PHP to demonstrate how a program would interface with an online database. We will discuss some interesting tools to manage your MySQL databases from a GUI interface. Tools like PHPMyAdmin and a couple of other free tools available to manage MySQL databases

Database Access with PHP and MySQL

PHP access to a database is often done with two HTML documents. One document to allow the user to enter a request for information from a database, the other works on the server side that runs the PHP to process the request and generate and return the completed HTML document. The user side is usually simple HTML. We will be mainly concerned with the server side and the database connection, processing and generating the return HTML.

Watch Out!

Since we are working with text files, there are certain characters that have been reserved for HTML (>, <, ", and &). Yet we may need to include them in our content. A system of symbols have been developed to handle these situations:

If you need a greater than symbol use &gt
If you need a less than symbol use &lt
If you need an ampersand use &amp

Connecting to MySQL and Selecting a Database

The PHP function ***mysql_connect()*** connects a script to a MySQL server. The function requires three parameters: (1) the host that is running MySQL [localhost is the default]. (2) the username for MySQL, (3) the password.

The PHP function ***mysql_close()*** closes the database.

The PHP function ***mysql_select_db()*** selects the database and requires one parameter, the name of the database.

EXAMPLE:

```
$db = mysql_connect("localhost", "abc", "");
$dbpay = mysql_select_db("payroll");
```

Requesting MySQL Operations

MySQL operations are requested through the ***mysql_query()*** function. Typically, the operation (a string literal) is assigned to a variable. The ***mysql_query()*** function uses that variable as a parameter.

EXAMPLE:
```
    mysql_query("INSERT INTO Friends (pID, fName, lName, Bday) VALUES ('1',
'Mike', 'Rowe', '1977-06-07')");
```

The mysql_fetch_array returns data from a table and stores the entire row in an array.

EXAMPLE:

```
for ($rown=1; $rown &lt;= $num_rows; $rown++)
    {
    $row = mysql_fetch_array($result);
    print "&ltp&gt Result row number ".$rown.". state_id: ";
    print htmlspecialchars($row["state_id"]);
    print "State: ";
    print htmlspecialchars($row["State"]);
    print "&lt/p&gt";
    }
```

mysql_fetch_array returns an array of the next row. The code example uses a for loop to loop through all of the records in a file. The output produced looks like:

state_id	state
1	Alabama
2	Alaska

Lesson 17.4 – Web Based Databases

Web Based Databases are becoming increasingly popular for distributing data over the internet. Even applications that were done in "in-house" database applications, are now being done with web based database products. The big advantage being that administration and maintenance of large, complicated databases can be a very complex operation. High end hardware, complicated database administrator tasks can be very costly. Then, throw in the cost to back up, hardware and personnel costs, space costs, software costs and we have what may be a very expensive operation. Then a sick employee or an employee that finds another job, that are in key positions may make bigger problems than many organizations are willing to suffer. This creates organizational and budgetary problems, especially for smaller organizations who cannot support the personnel and equipment overhead to support in house systems.

Enter web based databases. Put all of this responsibility on someone else. It makes the entire operation more affordable because the large costs of hardware, personnel and redundancy in both in an organization who can split this between many different customers. They may also provide expertise in the application area that may not be found in the smaller organizations.

We have discussed several applications that use web based databases like Amazon, Google, eBay, etc. and there are thousands more on the internet. However, the internet sites you see are but a fraction of the databases out there. Many are only available to the subscriber organizations, protected by elaborate security and totally hidden from the casual internet browser or search engine.

If you have any thoughts about serious web development, you will need a good understanding of the SQL language, one or more programming languages and as many of the tools your brain can handle. The more databases, programming languages and tools you know, you will be available to accept more different projects. Not everyone will want a PHP / MySQL solution just because

140

that is what you know. Many potential customers will have their own ideas of what to use and they are writing the checks.

That being said, go out and experiment, practice and learn. Find a product, download and play with it. Create your own applications just to get the expertise. Remember, the time you spend in experimentation, the more proficient you will become.

Lesson 17.5 – Summary

Web Based Databases are becoming a standard in web site processing. Think of how many different sites are centered around a database. Google and the other search engines, Ebay and the other auction sites, many retail stores have their catalog and inventory online for you to make purchases. Your local auto parts store no longer have to look up parts for your car in a big catalog, they access an online database. These are just a few of the applications of online databases.

In Review:

1. Known as the "Duct Tape of the Internet"
    a.   PHP
    b.   Perl
    c.   JavaScript
    d.   Java
2. Combination of JavaScript and XML
    a.   Java
    b.   Rails
    c.   Ruby
    d.   AJAX
3. A web development environment built on Microsoft's Common Runtime Language.
    a.   AJAX
    b.   ASP.NET
    c.   XML
    d.   Rails
4. MySQL operations are requested through the _____ function.
    a.   mysql_query()
    b.   query()
    c.   query_mysql()
    d.   none of the above
5. Web based databases are used extensively by:
    a.   Amazon
    b.   Google
    c.   eBay
    d.   all of the above

Appendix

Appendix A – Changes to Server2Go for MySQL

When using Server2Go and MySQL you need to make a change so the databases created are not removed each time Server2Go shuts down. By default Server2Go removes any created databases in MySQL when it is shut down. To avoid the removal of created databases you need to make the following change:

1. Locate the file pms_config.ini in the Server2Go folder.
2. Find the line: LocalMirror=1
3. Change to: LocalMirror=0
4. If Server2Go is running, it must be restarted.
5. Now any databases created will be available each time Server2Go runs.

Appendix B – About the PHP Installation

When you need to know the details about your current PHP installation, a simple PHP program can be generated to show all details about the PHP installation and the PHP environment.

The Figure B.1 is the program to run the phpinfo() function that will display the current PHP environment. The Figure B.2 is the first screen of the resulting output.

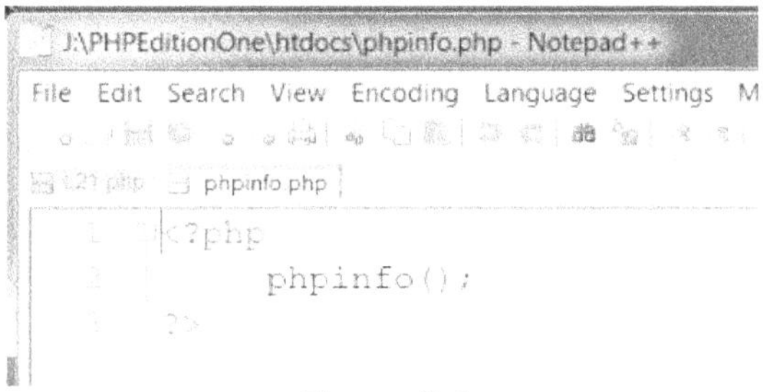

Figure B.1

The information covered includes:
      PHP Credits
      Configurations
            PHP Core
            Apache handler
            Apache variables
      HTTP Headers Information

      bcMath; calendar; com_dotnet; ctype; date; dom; filter; ftp; gd; hash; iconf; json; libxml; mbstring; mssql; mysql; mysqli; odbc; pcre; PDO; pdo_mysql; pdo_pgsql; pdo_sqlite; Reflection; session; SimpleXML; SPL; SQLite; standard; tokenizer; uddx; xml; xmlreader; xmlwriter; zlib

      Environment
      PHP Variables
      PHP License

The information includes the default values of many system variables, availability of various PHP extensions, linkages to databases and other essential information for PHP programmers.

PHP Version 5.2.10

System	Windows NT JIMK-PC 6.1 build 7601
Build Date	Jun 17 2009 16:16:01
Configure Command	cscript /nologo configure.js "--enable-snapshot-build" "--enable-debug-pack" "--with-snapshot-template=d:\php-sdk\snap_5_2\vc6\x86\template" "--with-php-build=d:\php-sdk\snap_5_2\vc6\x86\php_build" "--with-pdo-oci=D:\php-sdk\oracle\instantclient10\sdk,shared" "--with-oci8=D:\php-sdk\oracle\instantclient10\sdk,shared"
Server API	Apache 2.0 Handler
Virtual Directory Support	enabled
Configuration File (php.ini) Path	C:\Windows
Loaded Configuration File	C:\Users\jimk\AppData\Local\Temp\Server2Go_6248\php.ini
Scan this dir for additional .ini files	(none)
additional .ini files parsed	(none)
PHP API	20041225
PHP Extension	20060613
Zend Extension	220060519
Debug Build	no
Thread Safety	enabled
Zend Memory Manager	enabled
IPv6 Support	enabled
Registered PHP Streams	php, file, data, http, ftp, compress.zlib
Registered Stream Socket Transports	tcp, udp
Registered Stream Filters	convert.iconv.*, string.rot13, string.toupper, string.tolower, string.strip_tags, convert.*, consumed, zlib.*

Figure B.2 is only the first page of the phpinfo() printout, the PHP Credits.

Figure B.2

144

Appendix C – List of Escape Characters

Excape sequences are the combination of the escape character (the backslash \ ) which is used to signify the next character should be handled differently.

\"	Print the next character as a double quote.
\'	Print the next character as a single quote.
\n	Print a new line character (place the cursor at the beginning of the next line
\r	Print the carriage return.
\$	Print the next character as a dollar sign
\t	Print the tab character. Go in one Tab Stop.
\\	Print the next character as a backslash (\)

Appendix D – List of Reserved Words

abstract	and	array()	as	break	callable
case	catch	class	clone	const	continue
declare	default	die()	do	echo	else
elseif	empty()	enddeclare	endfor	endforeach	endif
endswitch	endwhile	eval()	exit()	extends	final
finally	for	foreach	function	global	goto
if	implements	include	include_once	instanceof	insteadof
interface	isset()	list()	namespace	new	or
print	private	protected	public	require	require_once
return	static	switch	throw	trait	try
unset()	use	var	while	xor	yield

A list of some of the more commonly used reserved words.

Start Programming with PHP

Practice Programming Projects

The best way to learn any programming language is to write programs. This section provides ideas for projects for you to program. See how many of these projects you can solve with what you have learned. Read each one carefully and plan your approach to solve the problem. These are all business / personal type projects from everyday problems.

Project 1	– Lumber
Project 2	– Shoe Store
Project 3	– China Project
Project 4	– Planet Weight
Project 5	– Dog Years
Project 6	– Coins Weight & Thickness
Project 7	– Mortgage Calculator
Project 8	– Change Maker
Project 9	– Currency Converter
Project 10	– Random Numbers (Lottery Picker) (Guess the Number) (Dice)

Some of the project give you sample input and output, others do not. These exercises are for you to learn to program AND to do the design.

Some programs can be done several different ways. An example is that some programs can use arrays or put the information in a MySQL database. I highly recommend that you learn to write this program both ways. Explore different ways to write the various programs. Enhance the programs, add functionality, always try to make your program do more than the original design. Try things and if you wreck your program, I hope you learn something like what NOT to do in a program. This is software, you can't break anything.

Project 1 -

Lumber

The standard 2" x 4" board is not 2 inches by 4 inches. It may start that way but by the time the process is finished in producing the board it winds up smaller. Write a program that asks the user to select the lumber dimension and then displays the actual size in inches and metric. Use the following table for values:

Nominal	Actual	Metric
1" x 2"	3/4" x 1-1/2"	19 x 38 mm
1" x 3"	3/4" x 2-1/2"	19 x 64 mm
1" x 4"	3/4" x 3-1/2"	19 x 89 mm
1" x 5"	3/4" x 4-1/2"	19 x 114 mm
1" x 6"	3/4" x 5-1/2"	19 x 140 mm
1" x 7"	3/4" x 6-1/4"	19 x 159 mm
1" x 8"	3/4" x 7-1/4"	19 x 184 mm
1" x 10"	3/4" x 9-1/4"	19 x 235 mm
1" x 12"	3/4" x 11-1/4"	19 x 286 mm
2" x 4"	1-1/2" x 3-1/2"	38 x 89 mm
2" x 6"	1-1/2" x 5-1/2"	38 x 140 mm
2" x 8"	1-1/2" x 7-1/4"	38 x 184 mm
2" x 10"	1-1/2" x 9-1/4"	38 x 235 mm
2" x 12"	1-1/2" x 11-1/4"	38 x 286 mm
3" x 6"	2-1/2" x 5-1/2"	64 x 140 mm
4" x 4"	3-1/2" x 3-1/2"	89 x 89 mm
4" x 6"	3-1/2" x 5-1/2"	89 x 140 mm

This program can be done two different ways. Use arrays or put the information in a MySQL database. I highly recommend that you learn to write this program both ways.

Project 2 –

Shoe Store

A shoe store has asked you to provide a web program for their web site that allows users to get an estimate on the price of various sneakers. The store carries four brands of sneakers and each brand has four different types of sneakers: Basketball; Fitness; Running; and Walking.

Create a simple, easy to use interface for customers to obtain prices for various items carried by the store. The requirements for the program are as follows:

1. Allow the customer to select a brand. Only one brand selected at a time.
2. Then the customer will select the type of sneaker.
3. Allow the customer to enter a quantity.
4. The customer is then prompted to select either Adult or Children's sneakers.
5. The price is calculated using the price lists show below. The price list represents the store's cost for the sneakers, the customer should see a price 30% higher than the price shown in the price list.
6. The form should show a date and time.

Adult Price List

	Adidas	Converse	Nike	Reebok
Basketball	$80	$70	$125	$118
Fitness	$50	$45	$88	$92
Running	$90	$88	$105	$111
Walking	$80	$71	$79	$89

Children's Price List

	Adidas	Converse	Nike	Reebok
Basketball	$60	$65	$117	$106
Fitness	$35	$38	$104	$100
Running	$55	$62	$109	$110
Walking	$40	$45	$80	$95

This program can be done two different ways. Use arrays or put the information in a MySQL database. I highly recommend that you learn to write this program both ways.

Project 3 -

China Project
A local fine china store has contracted you to write a program that will allow customers to enter the Brand and the quantity of an item and receive a price quote. The interface should be attractive and easy to use for the customer. This is their first step into an online presence and later they hope to make this a E-Store.

Basic system requirements are as follows:
1. Allow the customer to choose among the 5 brands of china: Mikasa, Noritake, Farberware, Royal Daulton, and their house brand Ironstone.
2. Each brand can have 5 component pieces; Bowl, Butter Plate, Cup, Plate, Saucer. The customer may order 1 or more of the component pieces.
3. The customer can choose the number of place settings (all 5 pieces) that they wish, but they can only order quantities of 1, 2, 4, 6, or 12.
4. When the customer chooses a brand, the component pieces, and the number of place settings, the price of the selected items should be displayed.
5. If the customer forgets to select a brand, a number of place sittings or at least one component piece, then an error message should be displayed and the cursor positioned to reenter the missing information.
6. After verifying that the customer has provided the application with all needed information, a calculated price should be displayed.

China Price Matrix

Brand	Piece	List Price		Brand	Piece	List Price
Mikasa	Bowl	$12		Royal Daulton	Bowl	$10
	Side Plate	$4			Side Plate	$8
	Cup	$6			Cup	$5
	Plate	$18			Plate	$6
	Saucer	$4			Saucer	$3
Noritake	Bowl	$6		Ironstone	Bowl	$1
	Side Plate	$2			Side Plate	$2
	Cup	$3			Cup	$3
	Plate	$9			Plate	$4
	Saucer	$2			Saucer	$2
Farberware	Bowl	$5				
	Side Plate	$3				
	Cup	$4				
	Plate	$8				
	Saucer	$3				

If you order a complete set (all 5 pieces) you must order in quantities of 1, 2, 4, 6, or 12.

150

Complete sets of 4 or 6 receive a 5% discount, sets of 12 receive a discount of 10%.

You are to come up with your original design with emphasis on visually attractive and user friendly.

This program can be done two different ways. Use arrays or put the information in a MySQL database. I highly recommend that you learn to write this program both ways.

Project 4 -

Planet Weight

The effects of gravity on various planets will affect your weight. Using Earth weight as our baseline for our weight, create a program that will ask for the users weight on earth and then determine the weight value for each of the other planets.

Planet	Multiply By
Mercury	0.37
Venus	0.88
Mars	0.38
Jupiter	2.64
Saturn	1.20
Neptune	1.12
Uranus	1.15
Pluto	0.04

SAMPLE INPUT

Enter the Weight on Earth: **189**

SAMPLE OUTPUT

```
Weight on Earth       189
Weight on Mercury     xxx
Weight on Venus       xxx
Weight on Mars        xxx
Weight on Jupiter     xxx
Weight on Saturn      xxx
Weight on Neptune     xxx
Weight on Uranus      xxx
Weight on Pluto       xxx
```

This program can be done two different ways. Use arrays or put the information in a MySQL database. I highly recommend that you learn to write this program both ways.

Project 5 -

Dog Years Converter

This program will calculate the number of months alive, given the years and the months old. The user enters the age in years and months and the program calculates and displays the number of months alive. Then calculates the age in dog years and displays that information also.

SAMPLE INPUT:

Age in Years: **15**
Months since last birthday: **3**

User enters 15 for years and 3 for months.

SAMPLE OUTPUT:

You are 183 months old

In Dog years your age is 76.3 years old.

Project 6 -

Coins - Weight
You have saved coins in a big jar. Now it is time to cash in. Counting all those coin will be a big pain but you want to have some idea how much you have saved before going to the bank. You researched the weight of coins and found the following table on the internet.

Denomination	Weight	Thickness
$0.01	2.500 grams	1.52 millimeters
$0.05	5.000 grams	1.95 millimeters
$0.10	2.268 grams	1.35 millimeters
$0.25	5.670 grams	1.75 millimeters
$0.50	11.340 grams	2.15 millimeters
$1.00	8.1 grams	2.00 millimeters

You decide to sort your coins by denomination and then weigh the pennies, nickels, dimes, quarters, half-dollars, and dollars and use their weight and the above table to calculate the approximate value of the coins.

Write a program that asks the user for the denomination, the total weight of the coins of that denomination, and the program calculates how many coins and their approximate value. The program displays the value of the coins and asks for the next denomination. When the user quits the program, a table is displayed with the denomination, the number of coins, and the value. The program will also display the total value of all the coins.
NOTE: Multiply Ounces by 28 to get Grams.

Coins – Stacks
You have saved coins in a big jar. Now it is time to cash in. Counting all those coin will be a big pain but you want to have some idea how much you have saved before going to the bank. You researched the thickness of coins and found the following table on the internet.

Denomination	Weight	Thickness
$0.01	2.500 grams	1.52 millimeters
$0.05	5.000 grams	1.95 millimeters
$0.10	2.268 grams	1.35 millimeters
$0.25	5.670 grams	1.75 millimeters
$0.50	11.340 grams	2.15 millimeters
$1.00	8.1 grams	2.00 millimeters

You decide to sort your coins by denomination and then measure the stacks of the pennies, nickels, dimes, quarters, half-dollars, and dollars and use their thickness and the above table to calculate the approximate value of the coins.

Write a program that asks the user for the denomination, the height of the stack of the coins of that denomination, and the program calculates how many coins and their approximate value. The program displays the value of the coins and asks for the next denomination. When the user quits the program, a table is displayed with the denomination, the number of coins, and the value. The program will also display the total value of all the coins.
NOTE: Divide Inches by 0.039370 to get Millimeters.

This program can be done two different ways. Use arrays or put the information in a MySQL database. I highly recommend that you learn to write this program both ways.

Project 7 -

Mortgage Calculator

Write a program to calculate the Monthly Payment for a mortgage using the following information:
Principal Amount
Interest Rate
Term (length of loan 30 years, 20 years, 10 years)

Use the Formula:
Monthly Payment = Principal * MonthInt / (1-(1/(1+MonthInt)) ^ (Years * 12))

MonthInt = Interest Rate / 12

The user enters the information into a form. Enter the Principal Amount in Dollars and Cents, the Interest Rate as a decimal (EXAMPLE: 3.95% entered as .0395) and the term which can be 30 years, 20 years or 10 years. The program should validate the data in all three entries.

The Monthly Payment should be calculated and displayed as shown below.

SAMPLE OUTPUT:

Amount Borrowed: $100000
Interest Rate: 3.95%
Term: 30
Monthly Payment: $000.00

Project 8 -

Change Maker

Develop a program that allows the user to enter a sale amount between $0.01 and $99.99. Then ask for a payment amount between $0.01 and $100.00. Then ask the user for the change due. The program should calculate the change due and if the user entered the correct amount, display the users estimate, the actual amount and if they match print "CORRECT!". If the amounts do not match print the message "TRY AGAIN!".

SAMPLE INPUT:
```
        Amount of Sale:        79.59
        Cash Tendered:         100.00
        Estimated Change Due:  21.41
```

SAMPLE OUTPUT:
```
        Your estimate was      21.41
        Actual                 21.41
                        CORRECT!              Or if not correct: TRY AGAIN!
```

Then ask the user how many of each denomination should be returned in change. Denominations of $50; $20; $10; $5; $1; $0.50; $0.25; $0.10; $0.05; and $0.01 may be used. The program should calculate the optimum denominations to make the change and compare to what the user selected. If a match, Congratulations, if not a match, TRY AGAIN!

SAMPLE INPUT   SAMPLE OUTPUT

AMOUNT: 21.41

Denomination		You	Computer
$50	0	0	0
$20	1	1	1
$10	0	0	0
$5	0	0	0
$1	1	1	1
$0.50	0	0	0
$0.25	1	1	1
$0.10	1	1	1
$0.05	1	1	1
$0.01	1	1	1
CORRECT!			

Project 9 -

Currency Converter

Write a program that asks for a whole dollar amount from the user and select the foreign currency from a list. Then does a currency conversion from US Dollars entered to the currency selected. Use the following table for conversion factors.

Currency	Conversion Factor
Euro	0.730
English Pound	0.595
Japanese Yen	101.545
Russian Ruble	34.745
Mexican Peso	12.893
Canadian Dollar	1.086
Korean Won	1,024.100
Norwegian Krone	5.934

Some variations to this program are:
1. Put the table in an array.
2. Put the table in a file.
3. Convert from the foreign currency to US Dollars.
4. Select a from currency and a to currency and convert.
5. Get additional conversion factors and include more currencies.

Project 10 -

Random Numbers (Lottery Picker) (Guess the Number) (Dice)

Project A – Simple Dice Game

In the text there is an illustration of a program that rolls two dice, and totals the two amounts. Use this as a basis for a program for two players. Players alternate turns and the sum of each roll is added to a counter. The first one to reach 100 wins the game.

Project B – Guess the Number

In this project the computer selects a random number between 1 and 100. The user is then prompted to guess the number. If the guess is too low the program should respond "LOW" and allow another guess. If the guess is too high the program should respond "HIGH" and allows another guess. If the user guesses the number print out a message of success and the program ends.

Project C – Lottery Picker

Lottery games like Powerball and Mega Millions are played by millions of people. Some have their magic numbers, others just let the computer pick their numbers. Write a program for Powerball or Mega Millions, using their number rules. The program should allow the user to pick numbers for one to twenty tickets.

www.ingramcontent.com/pod-product-compliance
Lightning Source LLC
Chambersburg PA
CBHW080419060326
40689CB00019B/4304